Scent of the Soil

Books by the same author

Indian Memsahib
Memsahib's Chronicles
Women Extraordinaire

Scent of the Soil
A CIVIL SERVANT RETURNS TO HIS ROOTS

Suchita Malik

Published by
Rupa Publications India Pvt. Ltd 2017
7/16, Ansari Road, Daryaganj
New Delhi 110002

Sales Centres:

Allahabad Bengaluru Chennai
Hyderabad Jaipur Kathmandu
Kolkata Mumbai

Copyright © Suchita Malik 2017

This is a work of fiction. Names, characters, places and incidents are either
the product of the author's imagination or are used fictitiously and any
resemblance to any actual person, living or dead, events or
locales is entirely coincidental.

All rights reserved.
No part of this publication may be reproduced, transmitted,
or stored in a retrieval system, in any form or by any means,
electronic, mechanical, photocopying, recording or otherwise,
without the prior permission of the publisher.

ISBN: 978-81-291-3545-2

First impression 2017

10 9 8 7 6 5 4 3 2 1

The moral right of the author has been asserted.

Printed in India by Replika Press Pvt. Ltd India

This book is sold subject to the condition that it shall not,
by way of trade or otherwise, be lent, resold, hired out, or otherwise
circulated, without the publisher's prior consent, in any form of binding or
cover other than that in which it is published.

*To emotions that get entangled in sarees and words,
and eventually overflow in tears and laughter;
and to words—little devils—whose perils and
pearls live on in memories for ever after...*

1

EVERYTHING WAS in order, nothing seemed amiss. The morning was particularly bright that late April day, and the sun shone in the azure sky, signalling an atmosphere of cheer and anticipation. A sense of excitement filled the air.

Vigyan Bhavan, the capital's pride and a symbol of independent India's power and glory, stood majestic as ever. It had been a witness to numerous great events in history and some exhilarating moments. It had served as a meeting point for respected thinkers and intellectuals as well as the powerful and the renowned. It had been the venue for some of the most significant political conclaves and consortiums of leaders from across the world. No wonder, then, that it was a highly sought-after rendezvous for facilitating a free flow of ideas, ideologies and philosophies. People came here with a sense of pride, commitment and wonder.

A warm glow pervaded the venue which was abuzz with activity. The auspicious day brought with it a promise of new beginnings for those about to gather here in a short while. For many, it might also signify the fulfilment of their aspirations and dreams.

Vigyan Bhavan bore a festive look. The fresh-flower decoration and flags added a tinge of colour and brightness to the building. An imposing board fixed above the entrance announced loud and clear: 'Civil Services Day, 21 April'.

Just inside the entrance was a raised, triangular platform,

which sported a lush display of small flowering shrubs, ferns and cacti of different hues. Arranged in an eye-catching pattern, the plants were outlined with pebbles, round and oval in shape and white in colour, highlighting the freshly painted white board that exhibited coffee-coloured designs on both sides. A single bee buzzed around, perhaps attracted by the vibrant display of flowers and their fragrance. The constant humming of the bee seemed to underline the flurry of activity that marked the opening of a new chapter in the administrative history of the country.

A carpeted path stretched out towards the few steps leading up to a magnificent door. At this entrance, stood ushers to check the invitations carefully. The door opened onto a spacious area where an aesthetic arrangement of books and reading material was slotted to catch everybody's eye. It also provided the perfect ambience for invitees to catch up with their colleagues, friends and peers. The mood was upbeat, eyes were full of pride and hearts were throbbing with anticipation. Families, dressed in vibrant colours to suit the importance of the occasion, looked elated as they talked and laughed loudly.

As the entrance hall began filling up with guests, mutual congratulations poured out of their twinkling eyes and overwhelmed hearts. Their ecstatic mood and feeling of camaraderie were enough to relegate the lines of hierarchy to the background. The all-powerful rungs of bureaucracy rubbed shoulders with one another in the otherwise reclusive atmosphere of the corridors of power.

'Where do we go from here? I mean, in the future?' wondered an officer.

'What do you mean?'

'I mean, the Prime Minister's Award is the highest recognition for a civil servant. What remains to be achieved?'

'An achievement gained and well appreciated is its own reward, Sir!'

'Our current administrative scenario doesn't lack in incentives, my dear man. Obstacles, as also their resolutions, are strewn in our path. One just has to take them up as challenges. One's zeal only determines one's resolve as well as its path.'

'Sir, can this award be won more than once?'

'Yes, why not? In fact, we have a couple of officers today for whom it is an honour won twice.'

'What luck, Sir!'

'Well, don't let the luck factor outweigh an officer's tireless efforts and determined, consistent approach. It has to be a combination of both.'

The light-hearted conversation came to an end with a request for everybody to occupy their seats in the main auditorium where the ceremony was to take place. They entered amid camera flashes. The atmosphere was upswing; the ushers were their most courteous self, and the officers were in a hurry to find their allotted seats and guide their family members to take their place. The momentum picked up when the compère's sweet, excited voice became audible to everyone. She was requesting everyone to calm down and settle in their respective seats.

'May I have your attention for a moment, please?'

The cheerful voices of the audience ebbed before the next announcement: 'The Hon'ble Prime Minister, our chief guest, is due to arrive shortly along with other dignitaries. We shall start the function at once after his arrival. Please settle down quickly and help us maintain the dignity of the house.'

The delegates, the participants and their guests nodded in tacit acceptance of the request. A few minutes ticked by quickly and then the hustle-bustle that precedes the arrival of the chief guest took over once again.

The Prime Minister, escorted by the Cabinet Secretary and the Secretary, Administrative Reforms, entered to the constant flash of camera bulbs. Everyone stood up as a mark of respect. The Prime Minister went up to the stage and everybody assumed their seats and sat in attention. All eyes turned towards the mistress of ceremonies as they waited for the programme to begin.

The arrangements on and around the stage had been kept simple and elegant. Each side of the stage was decorated with flowers, keeping the centre clear of all adornment. This would facilitate the awardees to reach the stage using the front steps and receive their citations and medals.

The flowers on both sides were roses: golden-yellow in colour and arranged in an upward slant that guided the eye straight towards the dais where the principal guests were seated at an antique oak table. The large yellow and orange backdrop sported a big insignia of the bureaucratic symbol, in deep rust and maroon colours. The ambience was perfect for such an august function, and so was the enthusiasm of all those present. Everyone waited for the proceedings to begin.

The opening ceremony was a routine affair: beginning with the welcome address, followed by reading of a report and the keynote address. The main event was the presentation of awards to those officers who could pride themselves on extraordinary achievements in the most difficult and adverse circumstances. They had dared to dream and had shown tenacity in overcoming challenges. Their endeavours had known no boundaries, their relentless spirit had shown no signs of slowing down or fatigue, their obsession for perfection and normalcy went hand in hand, and their idealistic streak had never been in abeyance. They held their heads high; their eyes sported a look that challenged the world at one glance; and their calm demeanour camouflaged a restless spirit and an unparalleled zeal.

The names of the awardees, individual or teams, were called out one by one. The announcer read out the list of their achievements and gave a brief outline of their careers. This was followed by the reading of the citation and the garlanding with the medal. The Prime Minister then handed over the Roll of Honour and said a few congratulatory words followed by a handshake as if to say, 'Well done, my champion! The world is at your feet... You are on top of your career today by the diligent and consistent observance of your duties, which you carried out in the gentlest manner but with an indomitable spirit... Bravo! Carry on, my most trusted lieutenant...'

The ceremony went by like a dream; the audience, as if entranced, clapped thunderously and endlessly. Their eyes were glued to the stage, their mouths were open in awe and wonder and their hearts were too full for words. Their eyes were moist, throats choked and their heads held high with pride. None wanted the moment to end.

The awardees, on the other hand, stood unassuming, but satisfied and with a look that spoke volumes. A dream had come true; something they had aspired to, conceptualized, and for whose success they had worked hard. Now, when it had become a reality, they stood mesmerized, unable to react or respond. Immersed in the solemnity of the moment, they wanted to cherish its memory for later introspection and relish. The moment itself was too delicious to savour amid public scrutiny. They wanted to enjoy it in the comfort of their homes, in the company of their soulmates and loved ones.

They accepted their awards and were later called in groups to pose for photographs. A few had received the awards in their individual capacity, many others were a part of a team. The elation, however, was unanimous and infectious. For those receiving the award for the first time, the moment was fixed indelibly in the deeper recesses of their hearts; something that would always be one of their most cherished memories.

But, there were others for whom it was an honour twice bestowed. They were indeed the rarest of the rare—champions who had achieved the mission impossible a second time. They, too, stood dumbstruck. They could hardly believe it. They were pleased, undoubtedly, but they tried to suppress the tinge of cynicism that naturally creeps in after having endured a lifetime of bureaucratic roller-coasting and administrative wrangling. But, all said and done, it had been a life well-spent, an award well-earned and well-deserved.

For them, it was a moment to look back on, introspect about and analyse, to ruminate over or even meditate on. The bureaucratic path had been one of excitement and inactivity, grit and glamour, remorse and retribution, sin and splendour.

'Do you regret anything?' asked their alter ego.

'No! Never! By no means! Our lives have been the envy of many. People would give their all to get even a glimpse of our well-guarded world.'

'Still, how do you feel?' insisted their alter ego.

'Tired, exhausted…mentally, physically and emotionally… taken to saturation point!'

The awardees stood straight, blasé, overcome! Their indomitable will, too, showed signs of slackening. The cracks in the steel frame of bureaucracy were in danger of being seen on the faces of some of the chosen ones.

2

Shubhojit Singh remained standing on the dais for a while, along with a few others, mulling over past events, trying to place things in perspective. He was a middle-aged, weary man who had travelled very far in search of greener pastures; in fact, the furthest possible since his adolescence and youth, when he had harboured dreams and had wanted to run fast to achieve them. He looked around with a gloomy curiosity; he saw pride and happiness on the faces of first-timers, and tried to look within himself to relive his own emotions when he had been one of them. He made a faint attempt to appear happy and satisfied, and put on a broad smile in order to camouflage his inner turmoil. But his eyes bore a look of restlessness and anxiety that is typical of a person who has run the longest race and won, but is still unsure of his victory.

'What a paradox! Why is happiness still eluding me? Why is my sense of achievement still incomplete? Where have I lagged behind?' wondered Shubhojit, lost in his own thoughts.

He kept looking down at the floor, unsure of his next move. 'I must get out of here as soon as possible,' he thought aloud, 'and allow others to celebrate the long-awaited moment.'

'Did you say something, Sir?' asked Adishankar, an officer standing next to him.

'Oh, no, not at all! Probably just blurted out a random thought. Not to worry!' said Shubhojit, his usually crisp voice dripping with boredom.

'Is there anything bothering you, Sir? Are you alright?' Adishankar was full of concern. 'Aren't you pleased, Sir? This is a repeat honour for you.'

Shubhojit looked at him with uncomprehending eyes. Adishankar ventured again, 'What a career, Sir! What a life! Full of achievements, recognitions and rewards! I am sure that every member of the service would be envious of your career!' Adishankar had sensed that something was amiss and made a vain attempt to lighten the mood.

Shubhojit made an effort to maintain a calm exterior; he knew very well that his dreams, fulfilled though they were, had somehow lost their sheen for him. He realized that the aspirations and achievements of civil servants, once fulfilled, were engraved in the minds of the following generations, who carried it forward in the form of a legacy.

'Yes, that's what has happened; it always happens and the achievers, sometimes, are left wondering whether the journey had been worthwhile in the personal context too.' Shubhojit, who was in no mood to allow anybody or anything to hamper his train of thought, told himself.

'I wish I had known when I was young that I would come this far,' said Shubhojit to Adishankar, turning towards him in an attempt to continue the conversation.

'Would it have made a difference, Sir? I mean, wouldn't it have taken the thrill away...the certainty of the future?' Adishankar ventured his view firmly and clearly.

'It would have saved me from making many mistakes, now that I can look back.' A feeling of regret had come into Shubhojit's eyes.

'Mistakes? I don't understand, Sir!'

'Well, nothing comes easy in this life, Adi! Or without

a price!' said Shubhojit. 'It is very difficult for men like me to strike a healthy balance between the personal and the professional life! By the time one finally understands the importance of maintaining this balance, one finds that the moment has been lost and one is left empty-handed. The seed of consequences has already been sown and one can do nothing about it except follow it to its logical end.'

'The logical end may be a relative term, Sir! The positive as well as negative connotations differ from person to person and, naturally, the circumstances too.'

Adishankar's tone, too, was getting sombre, synchronizing well with Shubhojit's mood.

The super achievers were all lined up on the stage; the photo shoot with the chief guest was in progress, different photographs from different angles would make eye-catching copy for the media and please all. The facial expressions of the civil servants were worth capturing: their body language told one story while their minds seemed to be elsewhere. Their eyes expressed an inner turmoil, though their lips divulged only what was politically correct. They were bound by a strange unity; disintegrated in their own selves, yet part of a whole. Each one seemed to be engrossed in the whirlpool of his own ideas. The flashing cameras diverted their minds, but only momentarily, and forced them to smile.

Shubhojit wanted to run away, run away from it all and go back. 'But go back where?' he wondered. Go back to the old times, to the carefree days of his youth when nothing had been certain or secure and yet he had breathed an air of freedom; where the simplicity of living had afforded a pleasure unknown to the élite or the wealthy and famous.

Adishankar, wishing to read Shubhojit's mind, was keen on

continuing the conversation; whether for sharing experiences or as a catharsis for his innermost thoughts, he himself did not know. The function had come to an end with the lunch. The chief guest was ready to leave. This was a clear enough signal for others to follow suit. Hugging each other warmly and saying goodbye to their colleagues, they came out under the porch. A whole range of red-beacon official cars waited upon them. They only had to give a signal to their drivers to bring the car to the spot.

Shubhojit and Adishankar had come out together and both were still keen on a conversation.

'Let's have a drink together, Sir!'

'Oh, sure!' said Shubhojit. 'Come along with me!'

'I shall follow you, Sir, in my own car. I do not want to inconvenience Ma'am.'

'I have come alone, come along!'

Adishankar sat in the car and looked at Shubhojit. 'Are you still thinking, Sir? You are upset on a day like this. Isn't it unusual?'

'Yes, Adi! I think that I was a happy man when I was a nobody. The path to glory, perhaps, dulls a man's innate goodness.'

'Sir, this is no day for such thoughts. Let's celebrate today!' Adishankar looked at Shubhojit.

'You know, Adi, when I did not have anything in material terms, I had everything that really mattered in life. Now, when I am at the pinnacle of my career, I am a pauper as far as my personal life is concerned. My wife has left me, and as far as my children are concerned, I am as good as abandoned by them. When they needed me, I was hardly ever there for them. Now, they don't need me anymore. My so-called successful career laid prior claims on my time and attention, and I always gave in. Now, when I want to be with them and long for their company, they no longer seem to be interested in me. Although professionally successful in society, I am absolutely unwanted in their eyes.' Shubhojit let out a sigh.

'Sir, the price of success is always very high. It takes its toll on us, in our professional as well as personal lives.'

While they were debating this question in the privacy of the car, they had reached their destination. The driveway was long and on either side there were beds of petunias, separated by shrubs. Beyond them, sprawled big, square lawns, beautifully manicured and offering a soothing green vista.

At the extreme corners of the lawns were spectacular arrangements of white stones, plants and seasonal flowers. The ground here was raised through a clever assortment of shrubbery, indigenous, sculpted artefacts and ferns. These broke the monotony of the green patch and could also be lit with fairy lights in the evening, giving the lawns a glowing, royal look.

Shubhojit guided Adishankar to the entrance of his house. The extended veranda, highlighting rust-brown tiles, stretched out on both sides of the main door. On it was a line-up of earthen pots, containing a wide range of flowers, perennial as well as seasonal. Beyond the veranda was a protective shed that housed a couple of personal cars: a comfortable sedan and a more dashing SUV, probably to suit different moods and occasions. The opening of the door produced a pleasant, tinkling sound, which came from a string of ghungroos strung across the top of the door, welcoming visitors.

The entrance lobby, though small, reflected the taste and lifestyle of the occupants. The atmosphere, as well as the placing of adornments, lent a touch of sophistication to it. A wood-framed print of Van Gogh's famous painting, *The Café Terrace at Night*, hung on the front wall that faced visitors as they entered. It set the tone for the decor rather well. The picture had a strange haunting quality about it. The deep blue sky was illuminated by glowing stars; an immense yellow lantern illuminated the terrace, the facade of the building, the side walk; small figures sat at tables and chairs on the terrace, giving the impression of a large, extended space. The painting was a clever portrayal of a café in the late evening. A few more such artefacts adorned the other walls: a traditional hanging Egyptian lamp gave out a soft, yellow-bronze light.

Shubhojit and Adishankar entered the drawing room, which opened out from the lobby. Adishankar looked around in admiration and was impressed by its imposing appearance. The furniture was simple and elegant; the furnishings, rich, and the curtains, thick and rich, provided a striking colour contrast.

The monotony of bare walls was carefully avoided by the placing of wall hangings: a Satish Gujral painting looked straight at you from the wall up front while Leonardo da Vinci's *Mona Lisa* smiled mysteriously from the wall on the right; an excellent Jaipur painting declared its antiquity and Madhubani sketches from Bihar and a couple of Pattachitra paintings from Odisha brightened the room.

The room had French windows that opened straight onto the rear lawn that was as beautiful and manicured as the front one, and twice as large. Against the rear wall, Adishankar could see a row of varicoloured bougainvillea providing a vibrant cover for it.

Shubhojit was keen to show him the fruit trees as well as

the kitchen garden. The jamun tree, he said, was of a unique variety and gave seedless fruit that had a rich, juicy pulp, which they shared generously with their neighbours. The bel tree was laden with fruit. There were various varieties of mango, guava and papaya trees which yielded ample fruit. The kitchen garden, too, was well kept and the vegetables grown were organic.

'Ma'am must be a very happy person! Also, she must take a lot of care of her plants!' said Adishankar.

Shubhojit was quiet for a few seconds before he blurted out impatiently, 'I told you before...I am separated from Yashodhra, and I live alone!'

'I am sorry, Sir! I had forgotten.'

'Let's have a drink and unwind!' said Shubhojit.

3

'What would you like to have, Adishankar?' Shubhojit glanced at him. 'Wine, whisky, anything else?'

'Anything, Sir! Whatever you offer!' smiled Adishankar.

'Glenfiddich or Chivas Regal or Black Label?'

'I would like the single malt and I take it on the rocks, Sir, if you don't mind!'

'Certainly, my dear man! You can have your choice at least in this. It is not an official issue.'

While Shubhojit poured out the drinks, he asked Bahadur, the cook-cum-bearer-cum-housekeeper, to serve a few snacks and sat down half-reclined on the sofa. He was in a mood to talk.

'How is life at your end, Adi? Tell me about yourself, your family and life with them.'

Adishankar smiled, picked up his glass and raised a toast. 'Here's to your success, Sir, and many more to come!'

Their glasses touched gently and Shubhojit said, 'Well, here's wishing much more success to you too, Adi! May you go far beyond where I have reached, and I wish you happiness in your personal life too!' He held out his hand and gave him a warm handshake.

'You know, Adi, I shall always remember this time, this particular day and the moment when you were here to celebrate my success with me. It has saved me from sinking into a fit of depression.'

'Sir, if I may take the liberty of saying so, you seem very disturbed today. Can I help you in any way? I shall deem it a privilege.'

The whisky was slowly warming up the atmosphere as well as the tone of their conversation.

'Adi, the world admires me for my achievements. I am a well-known man, almost a part of the VVIP club. Society holds me in high regard and envies my lot. But I am a lonely, dejected man today. I have nobody waiting for me when I return home in the evening, to comfort me after a gruelling day or to applaud me after a fruitful day.'

'Sir!'

Bahadur entered the room and set down the tray with the snacks. Shubhojit asked him to serve them and then leave. The two men enjoyed the sumptuous snacks along with sips of whisky and picked up the thread of conversation once again.

'Sir, can I ask you a question about something that has aroused my curiosity?'

'Yes, sure! Go on!'

'Sir, do you think that the compulsions of our professional lives make a serious dent in our personal lives? However hard we try, we can never come up to the expectations of our near and dear ones. Somehow, our efforts to fulfil their dreams always fall short.'

'Well, we can never be sure whether their dreams and aspirations are beyond our reach, or whether our desire to fulfil them takes a back seat in the face of unavoidable circumstances.' Shubhojit was slowly opening up.

'At times, we are losers on both counts. The responsibilities are always ours, in all situations. And, according to the general perception, we are deemed to have power in almost everything.

But, our families are invariably dissatisfied, no matter how hard we may try.' Adishankar, too, felt like confiding.

'You know, Adi, I always tried my best to fulfil my responsibilities—official as well as personal. I had to compromise with my principles and sense of idealism too at times to keep peace in the family.'

'How, Sir?'

'Right from the beginning, I was very particular regarding the use of my official car for family purposes. Then I compromised, but tried to keep it within the normal permissible limit. However, slowly, that started to become a sore point. The reasons, as cited by Yashodhra, were always the examples of others. "Look at the Bhutanis!" she would say. "Richa always has an official car at her command. She never uses her own vehicle. She wants a chauffeur-driven, red-beacon car to take her everywhere. Their children follow suit. What is wrong with that, tell me," she would argue. "You work almost from 9 a.m. to 9 p.m. At least do that to compensate for loss of family time."'

'Hm.'

'You know, Adi, she never tried to understand my point of view or respect my wishes. She was totally engrossed in keeping up appearances. Deprived of my company, she drifted away from our value system, enticed by the glamour and power that come with this coveted service.'

'Sir, children are usually the mute but perceptive spectators in any rift between husband and wife,' said Adishankar, thinking, perhaps of his own experience. 'They get confused and are left groping for their own set of values. We opted for a car-pool system in our lane where all the officers' children go to the same school, at almost the same time. But I must confess that it was difficult for our children, Anirudh and Aarti, to get used to the idea of sharing a vehicle. Children of that age are susceptible to peer pressure, and they need our constant guidance.'

'Difference of opinion between husband and wife,' said Shubhojit, 'can take a toll on children's upbringing. Our constant and long absences from home don't make it easier for the family. Yashodhra and I started out well. In fact, ours was a love marriage. We survived all pressures and stuck to each other. The intensity of our feelings and the somewhat similar ideology gave us strength all through. It was a blissful and near-perfect companionship at the outset. We loved doing things together. The intimacy and the togetherness, the first taste of power, the new life, and the excitement of the excellent future prospects brought stars in our eyes. It was overwhelming and we felt blessed.'

'Sir, you seem to be a romantic at heart. The clarity with which you describe your emotions and thoughts of earlier times says a lot about your heartfelt sentiments.'

'Adi, that is, in fact, the travesty of our job and the tragedy of our lives. Romance, love, intimate moments with the family, aspirations, longings, convictions and even idealism get sacrificed at the altar of the bureaucratic pedestal that only looks at you, smiles, mocks and remains indifferent.'

'Sir, you have touched a raw nerve,' said Adishankar.

'Can I pour you another drink? And yes, let's have some more snacks.' Shubhojit got up, made him a drink and offered a plateful.

Looking in the direction of the kitchen, Shubhojit called out, 'Bahadur! Please get us some more snacks.' Bahadur appeared quickly and responded, 'Yes, Sahib!'

'Adi, tell me about your wife, children and your family life. I hope it is smooth sailing for you. Your children must still be studying.'

'Sir, the grass always looks greener on the other side of the fence. I think we civil servants have to make a lot of adjustments in our personal lives. We have to be prepared to compromise our value system too, at times. We cannot always prevent our family members from wishing to have expensive new gadgets or dining frequently at high-end eating places.'

'Yes, one thing leads to another,' said Shubhojit, 'until it becomes a way of life for them and extremely difficult to check. The new-found status of our family members and the readiness of favour-seekers to oblige by catering to their seemingly innocuous initial demands set in motion a chain of events over which, later, we have no control.'

'And, Sir, all our attempts to check this trend are met with disapproval and a stiff behaviour. Our well-meant reproaches are treated with a subtle indifference. I once had a heated argument with Malini, my wife, over a dinner invitation. I wanted to decline it for a number of reasons. The invitation came from an industrial house with which I had an official relationship. They were in a mood to oblige but I was not willing to be pampered. Malini could not understand that I would have had to pay a price for this, at some point, in my career.'

'You are right.'

'"Why are you so unsocial, Adi?" she would often ask and throw a tantrum. "I am sick of being alone the whole day. Don't deny me the pleasure of an outing in the evening. Get ready, we are going, dear!" Malini would insist.'

'Sir, at times I agreed just to avoid the confrontations at

home. I would try to convince her that people always acted with a motive, and an invitation to a dinner was an investment for something we couldn't even guess. Our presence at their lavish get-togethers also gives them an opportunity to boast of their connections with us. But Malini would dismiss my arguments with an agitated sniff. I felt suffocated and found myself unable to drive home my point of view.' Adishankar's face bore a troubled look.

'Adi, I understand this very well. It never stopped there. Soon, our wives were being wooed by the spouses of these smart people who would show off their wealth, diamonds and high lifestyle.'

'Exactly, Sir! Even the most innocent minds can be influenced by such display of riches. At times, I didn't blame Malini; rather, I empathized with her. I could neither give her loads of money nor take her around the world for holidays. We couldn't even afford eating out at five-star hotels every now and then. I couldn't buy expensive gifts for her or give her a new car every time a new model came in the market. The rich, perhaps as compensation for lack of their company, indulge their wives with all these niceties. I could give Malini nothing; neither this nor my physical presence.' Adishankar sighed.

'Yes, Adi!' said Shubhojit. 'On top of that, we expect all kinds of compromises from them. I don't blame Yashodhra either. She tried her best. She allowed her career to take a back seat. She was always there for my family whenever they needed her. She looked after my relatives and took care of all my responsibilities. She doted on the children and was a very caring mother. She attended PTA meetings and was wholly in charge of their education. She took them to the doctor or the hospital whenever they were sick. She never burdened me with any of those responsibilities,' said Shubhojit in an emotional tone. 'And when I look back, I ask myself what I gave her in return. Did I try to make her life easy? Did I help her in any way or put myself in her shoes and try to see life from her perspective? No, Adi, I did nothing of the sort. Rather, I always tried to find fault with her system of functioning and imposed my own ideologies on her frail shoulders. No wonder she cracked under the pressure. And I realized my folly only when it was too late.' Shubhojit's eyes were moist as he took a long draught of whisky.

'Sir!'

'You know, Adi, Yashodhra left me for another man…far below me in status and rank…but one who could give her what she wanted in life.' Shubhojit wiped his moist eyes. 'You know what she said?'

'What, Sir?'

'"I didn't want your Prime Minister's Award for companionship, Shubhojit. I have always wanted you…and you alone…but you never understood. Let me go! I have outgrown my feelings for you." And she slammed the door in my face and walked out. I felt my awards and trophies mocking me, unable to give me solace or peace of mind.' Shubhojit tried hard to control his feelings.

4

ADISHANKAR TOOK his leave soon after and Shubhojit was left alone. He remained immersed in his thoughts for some time. No one came to disturb him or offer a kind word or gesture. Bahadur cleared the empty glasses and plates without a word. He was used to his master's mood swings and moments of withdrawal. After a while, he came back and asked hesitantly, 'What shall I make for dinner, Sahib? I hope you are having it at home.'

'Don't bother about it, Bahadur! I am not hungry,' Shubhojit said dismissively.

'Don't neglect your health, Sahib! You are not eating properly nowadays,' Bahadur continued. 'Today is a great day in your life, Sahib! I wish the whole family had been here, just like in happier times.'

Bahadur had been with Shubhojit for the last twenty years and was almost like a member of the family.

Shubhojit ignored his words with a smile and asked him to go to his quarters. 'I shall call you if I need anything. Meanwhile, wind up your work and leave some fruit on the table.'

Bahadur left with a resigned air. Shubhojit's mind could not but go back to his comment, '…just like in happier times.'

'Ah yes…happier times!' thought Shubhojit. 'How real they seem even today! I wish we human beings realized how quickly they can pass away. Yashodhra, oh my sweet darling

Yashodhra, why the hell did you…? Why didn't you understand that I loved you so much? Why did love have to be articulated always? Why don't our loved ones understand the intensity of our feelings? Oh, sweetheart, how could you do this to me?' Shubhojit's emotions were in a tumult and his thoughts rushed unabated. 'Perhaps it was more of my fault, dear! I took you for granted…everything: your feelings, professional life, likes, dislikes, convenience, time, in fact, your entire life.' Shubhojit's eyes turned towards the family portrait, a souvenir from bygone times that seemed to him an entirely different era now. It had become a priceless keepsake for Shubhojit since then.

Shubhojit's gaze was fixed on Yashodhra's lovely face. She was dressed in a rose-pink Banarasi saree with an all-over paisley motif. Her voluminous, shoulder-length hair was brushed back and complemented the gentle look on her face. She wore a delicate necklace and long, dangling earrings. Her eyes wore an affectionate and sweet look. She looked gorgeous by the side of a beaming Shubhojit, their children on either side. The photographer had caught a perfect, 'happy family' moment and the intrinsic quality of their sentiments.

A wave of nostalgia and remorse washed over him. His mind was in a tizzy; past events, occasions and happenings swirled before his mind's eyes; he was overwhelmed by the sheer force of the truth that danced before him and sent his emotions into a whirl. He recalled several incidents and his initial warm relationship with Yashodhra, Neelakshi and Hemant, though it ended in bitter fights too many times. They would all sit up in bed, order food from outside and watch TV together. It offered a break from the monotonous routine and the regular home food.

One particular night, Bahadur was away and they decided to order in Chinese food. They decided to watch TV and eat together, the four of them; the children enjoyed it. Yashodhra had set a few rules for the family. As Shubhojit was usually late for dinner and the children missed their quality time with him, she had made it obligatory for all of them to eat together at least twice a week and catch up on each other's lives.

'This way, Hemant and Neelakshi will remain connected with you, Shubhojit,' she reasoned with him. 'And you will also experience the pleasure of seeing your children grow up. Don't miss out on their childhood, dear!' Yashodhra would coax him.

'But why do we have to eat sitting in bed, Yashodhra? It is messy and also uncomfortable! It puts them into bad habits. There's a right way to do things. Why can't you teach them tradition and etiquette? Isn't that your responsibility?'

'Are the responsibilities all mine? Don't you too have a role to play in the family?' fumed Yashodhra.

'What do you mean? I try to do my best. Tell me, where do I lag behind?'

'How much time do you spend with your children? I insisted upon this arrangement because I want to see the family together at least at dinner time. Neelakshi and Hemant enjoy watching their favourite TV programmes. I thought if we could all eat together and watch TV, we could participate in their enjoyment.'

'Being addicted to TV at this age is definitely wrong. It will affect their studies.'

'You can't stop that altogether for them. One has to keep pace with the times and allow children some freedom,' said Yashodhra.

'One bad habit will lead to another till it reaches a point from where there is no going back.'

'It is easier said than done, Shubhojit!' said Yashodhra. 'Why can't you come home on time in the evenings and monitor their activities, sometimes, at least?'

'Let's not go there again, Yashodhra!'

Neelakshi and Hemant ate busily, their eyes glued to the television, spilling bits and pieces of food on the bed.

'Mom, can you get the chocolate mousse from the fridge, please?' yelled Hemant, licking his lips which were smeared with chilli sauce.

'Why can't you get it yourself instead of ordering your mother?' shouted Shubhojit, looking angrily at him.

'Oh, please, Papa! You will never understand this. It is so much more fun when we eat our dinner alone with Mom.'

'You should sit at the table and have your meals. Also, restrict your TV time. Your exams are drawing close!'

'Oh, Papa, do let us mind our own business while you mind yours in office,' shouted Hemant and looked away. Shubhojit was extremely angry while Yashodhra and Neelakshi watched the exchange of words between father and son.

'Is this the way to behave, Hemant? Since when have you become so disrespectful to elders? Is this what you have learnt from your school and your family?'

'What family are you talking about Papa? I hardly see you at all, anywhere...school, home or elsewhere. I only see my mother slogging around the whole day. You have never really cared for us or our needs or hopes. Have you ever bothered to ask what we want to do in life? Have you ever been present on any of those days that are important to us? No, Papa, you are lacking in your duties as much as we are lacking in good behaviour,' Hemant retorted.

'In fact, this evening,' said Neelakshi, 'has been a sort of punishment for all of us.'

'Will you both shut up or would you like a slap?' shouted Shubhojit, furious and unable to control himself. 'Yashodhra, are these the manners you have taught our children?' Shubhojit's anger turned towards his wife.

'Oh, you too shut up!' Tears rolled down Yashodhra's face.

'What did you say?'

'I said, "Shut up!"'

Shubhojit got up, picked up paper napkins and wrappers of snacks from the floor and left the room without saying anything. Not a word was uttered in the house by anyone for an hour or so. Soon, it was time for Yashodhra to put away things, say goodnight to the children and come back to their bedroom. She dreaded the moment when she would have to face Shubhojit again and they would continue their fight. She entered quietly and looked defiantly at Shubhojit. She was in no mood to reconcile; rather, she watched him with scorn. Whenever they fought or had any difference of opinion, it was left to Shubhojit to make the first conciliatory move. But this time, he was in a mood to talk and talk serious.

'Isn't anyone ashamed of what happened in this house today?' asked Shubhojit, trying hard to compose himself.

'A climax is usually the culmination of a long lull and a simmering within. I hope you do agree, Shubhojit.'

'Why don't you understand? I always try my best. You have to appreciate that my official duties are not the same as those of an ordinary man. You have been my main support system uptill now and you have been so good. What has suddenly gone wrong? I am shocked by the way the children talked. I am a defeated man, Yashodhra.'

'Why don't you look within yourself and figure out how well you know your children. What do you share with them on a daily basis? You have been so busy in your work that they have literally grown up without your influence. I think that Hemant is going astray. I don't like the company he keeps. He doesn't mix with the right kind of boys. I have warned him a couple of times but I feel he is easily attracted to bad influences.'

'Why didn't you tell me earlier?'

'You were hardly in a mood to listen. Besides, you get into a sermonizing mode. Children are not willing to listen to lofty words. They want their parents to be friends and share their interests and concerns. They don't want to listen to the ideologies of the golden past. They want to live in the present and act according to the times. You need to deal with them patiently. In fact, one needs to grow along with them,' said Yashodhra.

'What bullshit!'

'Yes, that's your problem, Shubhojit. Everything that is not pleasant to your ears is bullshit. That's why you are a stranger to your own children. You have never known them nor will you ever get to know them. I have put up with you and your rigid, obsolete ideas. Many women, in my position, go ahead in life on their own terms. They don't sit and wait upon their men to treat them the way they want to.'

'What has happened to all of you? I slog day and night for my family. I am horrified by their sheer hostility towards me. The list of your demands increases at the same speed as I go down in your esteem.' Shubhojit's words betrayed his hurt feelings.

Shubhojit and Yashodhra went on and on, unmindful of the pain they were causing to each other by their use of spiteful, hate-filled words.

'Why don't you leave me and go your own way, Yashodhra, as you just said?' shouted Shubhojit. 'Try to earn a living and you will find that life is not a bed of roses.'

'You will be sorry for your words one day, Shubhojit, mark my words!' Yashodhra wiped her tears and ran out of the bedroom.

The sound of an opening door brought Shubhojit back to reality.

5

Shubhojit got up and drew back the curtains. The evening was slipping into darkness and the faint glimmer of twinkling stars was becoming visible. The air was filled with the shrill, twittering noise of birds who were, perhaps, returning to their nests. Still immersed in the reverie, the sounds were unpleasant to him. They filled him with anguish. A deep feeling of dissatisfaction crept through him and he knew that all his efforts to overcome it would be futile.

'I can't let myself down this way,' thought Shubhojit, 'it is Saturday evening and the last thing I want to do is to sit at home and mope. Life is still full of possibilities for me and I can find myself any company that I want.' Shubhojit poured himself another drink and put on his favourite music.

'I shall listen to some old, romantic songs and pull myself out of this dismal mood. Ah, my favourite whisky, my age-old sweetheart, you will never desert me, come what may! I can be myself and open my heart in your company. You understand me well, as always.' Shubhojit's spirits were reaching the exhilarated heights that naturally follow a higher-than-usual intake of alcohol.

The melodious, old Hindi songs lifted his sagging morale; the notes were lilting, the words coquettish but meaningful and the voice of the singer inviting and soothing. It made him feel young again: youthful, romantic and carefree, someone for whom life still held the promise of a bright future.

'Oh! There is no substitute for youth,' he almost thought aloud. 'Youth can be so wild. How raw and inexperienced we were then! Life was so interesting, filled with fun, food, girls, movies, going to hangouts, going to college etc. The uncertainty of the future did not bother us. Relationships could be sweet or sour, and heartbreaks were temporary. There was always a new prospect looming large around the corner.' Shubhojit took several sips of whisky. 'Why does the thrill and excitement of youth get buried in the trivialities of ordinary family life? Why don't I still have that carefree attitude? Why has it been replaced with restlessness?'

The sound of music brought Bahadur back to the drawing room and he was surprised to see his master still drinking.

'Sahib, would you like something to eat? I can make a sandwich!'

'No, I am fine. I'll go, have a shower and get ready. I am going to the officers' club to join my friends over a game of cards and drinks. I shall not be having dinner at home. And yes, I might be late; don't wait up for me. You can go to sleep, the guard will open the door for me.'

'Sahib, so much drinking is bad for your health!'

Shubhojit laughed aloud—the first time during the evening—and looked at him affectionately. He gave him a pat on his shoulder and smiled. 'Bahadur, don't you ever try to get into the role of a wife. I don't want to lose you too, my friend!'

The evening's festivities were in full swing by the time Shubhojit reached the officers' club. His spirits greatly perked up at the sight of the impressive lobby, the bright illumination of the yellow lights, the huge crystal chandeliers which added to and reflected the glow and the mirthful chatter of the assembled people. Cascading water arrangements in the middle of the room added softness as well as a soothing coolness to the ambience. Gone were his dismal mood, his inane ideas and the thought of irritating problems. A feeling of belonging and a sense of bonding with the civil service fraternity brought an instant cheer to his mood. He was at once welcomed by loud greetings from almost everyone, who congratulated him profusely on being conferred the coveted PM's award for the second time; a rare achievement even among the most talented ones.

'Congratulations, Shubhojit! May you win more accolades in future and become an icon in the history of our service,' were the unanimous words of approval and appreciation.

Shubhojit was the hero of the hour. Good wishes greeted him everywhere he chose to cast a glance. He was enveloped in an aura of awe, and people looked at him as if he were the epitome of achievement. The choicest of drinks were doing the rounds and the members had decided to cast off their inhibitions and pressures and the insipidity of their routine official life. The officers raised a toast in his honour.

'Here's to our most celebrated hero!' said one with the utmost respect.

'Here's to the long life of our champion!' said another one.

'Here's to his long-lasting happiness...'

The club was full of officers, their spouses and children. The night was still young; drinks were flowing freely; the snacks on offer were lip-smacking and piping hot; peppy music invigorated the atmosphere and the civil servants were in a mood to talk, listen and dance.

Shubhojit was led to the dance floor by some younger members of the service. 'Sir, you can't refuse today! It is our privilege!'

Foot-tapping music was put on and beautiful young ladies in colourful, contemporary clothes circled round Shubhojit and asked him to dance with them. The male members looked on, clapping and laughing!

The younger ones set the ball rolling and a lady wearing a shimmering gown came forward to offer her hand to Shubhojit for a dance. He was obliged to accept and he gracefully took to the floor with the ravishing beauty, who was followed by another, and yet another, till all the officers joined in, paired up with their spouses and encircled Shubhojit who had, by now, gotten into a 'high' mood, given the intake of liquor and the vibrancy of the moment. The spontaneous dancing continued for about half an hour when Shubhojit spotted a large table where his colleagues seemed to be engaged in a lively discussion. They waved at him.

'Hey, Shubhojit…what's up? Let's have another drink.'

'What's the latest news? What have you been laughing about? I have been watching you for some time.' Shubhojit settled himself with another whisky and soda.

'Kanwaljit seems to have landed himself in trouble. Have you heard?'

'What has he done?' Shubhojit was curious.

'A video clip with objectionable stuff has gone viral. It is all over social media. Haven't you seen it, Shubhojit?' asked Manreet, a batchmate.

'Is it genuine or a concocted one?' asked Shubhojit. 'You can never tell these days.'

'I haven't seen it yet,' said Nagpal. 'What does it show? Do tell.'

'A group of people dancing, drinking, talking in intimate, hushed tones with curtains drawn, and the light, extremely dim.'

'Perfect romantic moments…after a hard day at office.' The laughter was mischievous.

'Hey, young boy, fill our glasses, please!' Devashish called out.

'Does it identify the people involved?' asked Shubhojit. 'Or is there any room for the benefit of doubt?'

'I am sure the faces must be slightly visible or they wouldn't have been asked to explain,' continued Manreet. 'Besides, somebody has filed a case in court for petty reasons, just to embarrass, it would seem.'

'The case has been moved to another jurisdiction to ensure transparent proceedings, apparently at the behest of the complainant.'

'It is also alleged,' said Nagpal, 'that the people involved were being pressurized to reach a compromise.'

'There must be another side to the story as well,' smiled Shubhojit. 'It is a pity that dirty linen has to be washed in public.'

'The officer's lawyer has alleged that the case was filed only to extort money. Otherwise, they would not have resorted to such measures.'

All the officers nodded and seemed to agree.

'Well, there are always people—including women—ready to lure officers using their resources and charms, and blackmail them later to meet their personal agenda.'

'The modus operandi is first to ensnare the powerful and then use threats to expose them if they don't dance to their tune!'

'There is a rumour that they are asking for a handsome amount to settle the matter.'

'Imagine their cheek and audacity!' said Devashish.

'Why do people fall into their trap?' asked Manreet. 'Are

they so naive that they can't see it is a bait?'

'The complacency of power,' said Shubhojit, 'combined with the easy access to forbidden goods!'

'A deadly combination that can ruin a life and wreck family peace,' said Nagpal.

'The persons involved are more to be blamed in this. As public servants, they are expected to maintain a dignified profile and clean image. They should not fall prey to such temptations or indulge in wayward behaviour, rampant though it is in our society.'

The fever of loud and heart-thumping music was catching. Young couples, oblivious to the mundane world around them, were lost in a world of their own. The dance floor was a getaway from routine. They held each other in their arms; their love-filled eyes spoke volumes about the intensity of their relationships; their bodies moving gracefully to the music. The atmosphere was enchanting and there was something for everybody. The alcohol flowed abundantly for those who cared to take it; the dance floor was like a dream sequence; delicious and mouth-watering snacks were offered to tingle taste buds and satiate hunger; the fragrance of the fresh flowers was sweetening the air. And there was a full moon which could be seen through the glass ceiling of the lobby.

The world of civil servants appeared glowing and beautiful. The privileged, élite section of society was a beaming mass of humanity. They talked, laughed, discussed, shared their experiences and looked for traces of happiness on each other's faces.

'Are they all really happy?' mused Shubhojit. 'Or is it really a facade? Are they privileged even in the enjoyment of small pleasures of life, unlike ordinary people? Would they display their real feelings in public and present themselves as absolutely human?'

'A penny for your thoughts, Shubhojit?' asked Manreet.

'At the age of fifty-six, I feel I am carrying the burden of bureaucracy like an albatross round my neck.' Shubhojit's unexpectedly bitter remark fell like a thunderbolt on his colleagues, and dashed their high spirits.

'Let's have dinner now! We are hungry!' They got up and walked towards the dinner table.

'Let's meet for a game of bridge tomorrow morning!' said Devashish.

'Sure!' said Shubhojit. 'We'll carry on the conversation we have left incomplete today.'

6

*T*HE HANGOVER from the previous night prevented Shubhojit from getting up early on Sunday morning. He decided against going for a walk since the sun was already fairly high up in the sky. This routine too could take a break for today, decided Shubhojit. He came out of his room. He wanted to have tea in the wide terrace outside it. He wanted to soak in the freshness of the morning, listen to the sweet kooh-kooh of the koel and bask in the fast-rising sun, which was filtering through the dense branches of the mango tree. He noticed that the blossom on the mango tree, which filled the air with a subtle, sweet smell sending the koel into raptures of ecstasy, had already started turning into tiny fruit.

Shubhojit took a deep breath and inhaled the fresh air. It helped him unwind and get over yesterday's gloomy memories of past happenings. Shubhojit watched a little bird come hopping into the terrace, perhaps looking for food. It had hunched-up shoulders and a small beak. It was a sparrow—a species that was fast diminishing in present times—he concluded. The bird's quick eyes, restless movement and constant twitter attracted Shubhojit. He wanted to listen to it, perhaps even talk. Birds have a strange power of understanding the human mind and its quirks, thought Shubhojit. And yes, the only thing they would want in return was, perhaps, a few pieces of bread if they were bold enough to come near you and take them. Shubhojit felt a strange bonding with the bird that sat at a distance and looked straight at him. He experienced the feeling of a peculiar connect or perhaps a longing for contact. Then, suddenly, the bird took wing, sped across and sat on a low branch of the mango tree. Shubhojit laughed, listened and waited for it to come back. But the bird's attention was fixed elsewhere and, after a while, it flew away.

It was past 7 a.m. and the air was getting a bit warm. Bahadur came looking for him, carrying the tea tray and some biscuits. It was a routine which he had observed since the early days of his career. Shubhojit liked having tea the proper way and Yashodhra had always understood and respected his wishes. His thoughts went back to the days when they used to sit on the terrace of their previous duplex house, half-shaded by the branches of a large mango tree that stood next to the boundary of the house. They would enjoy sipping English tea as they browsed through the morning newspapers. That was a time of deep love and understanding between them. The ritual of the early-morning tea had always been delightful. Tea, served in a teapot, would be left to brew for about ten minutes. The milk and sugar were served separately. There would be an assortment of biscuits. The leisure time would last for about half an hour till Yashodhra was needed to help the children get ready for school.

The morning time, though a bit rushed, had always been interesting and full of activity. The minutes would fly until it was time to leave for the office.

'Office!' thought Shubhojit, and came back to the present moment. The whole day stretched out ahead of him and he had to devise ways to keep himself busy. He went inside and brought out his pipe. He felt like smoking. It helped him think and relax but every time he smoked, the statutory warning came to his mind, 'Smoking Kills!'

'What does it matter?' smiled Shubhojit. 'Even though my life may be shortened by a few years, right now, it soothes my nerves and gives me pleasure.'

'Hey, Shubhojit!' came a few voices from the gate. 'We see the old rooster is up to mischief once again. Will you give us a cup of tea?'

Three of his batchmates were returning from their morning walk and had spotted Shubhojit sitting out and having tea.

'Oh, come in,' said Shubhojit. 'It is always a pleasure!'

More teacups were brought in and Bahadur was instructed to prepare breakfast for all of them.

'You can inform your families that I have kidnapped you for a couple of hours,' smiled Shubhojit.

The conversation veered round to the previous day's topic of people falling prey to temptations.

'Kanwaljit's case is just the tip of the iceberg, you know,' said Manreet. 'It is rather unfortunate. It is difficult to pinpoint the real victim.'

'Well, we have all kinds of people in our service. Sometimes, a slight incident may be blown out of proportion by the media. At other times, a group of people indulging in wrongdoing may go scot-free, using their influence and political clout,' said Devashish.

'Whom are you referring to, Devashish?' Nagpal winked at him.

'Well, all of us know whom we are talking about. Nothing remains a secret in our service for long,' said Manreet.

'It is a pity that such occurrences have become so common

these days,' said Shubhojit. 'When we joined the service, things such as one-night stands, live-in relationships, extra-marital affairs were unheard of. And if any such matter did become public knowledge, it was frowned upon.'

'Yes, I fully agree,' said Manreet. 'If there was the slightest trouble between an officer and his wife, the senior officers always considered it their moral responsibility to counsel the couple and sort out their differences.'

'Did it help?' asked Nagpal.

'Yes, it did! Most times! Our value systems were so different then. The younger generations are just not bothered about these things any more. I have come to know from reliable sources that their frequent visits to other posh metropolitan cities may not be as simple or innocuous as they always seem,' said Shubhojit.

'How do they maintain such extravagant living and ensure privacy in these things?'

'Well, they allow themselves to be hoodwinked into believing that matters go unnoticed.'

'There was a case about which I read recently in a newspaper. The man concerned kept a woman safely tucked away in another city. He made regular visits to her and pampered her to such an extent that she began to nurture dreams of having a permanent relationship and started pestering him.'

'Yes, she became too big for her shoes and the person concerned realized his folly only when it was too late.'

'He tried to reach a compromise with the woman,' said Nagpal, 'but her demands were too high and he turned them down. She filed a case against him in court for exploiting her and denying her legal rights.'

'It is another matter that the court deemed the relationship consensual since it had continued over a number of years,' said Shubhojit, 'but the damage done to his reputation was irreparable.'

'There have been many instances of the kind lately, right?'

'You know what they say? "Birds of a feather flock together." They hobnob with like-minded politicians and indulge in potentially dangerous liaisons. There is no dearth of pimps to supply liquor and willing women, with which they entice the hapless victim until he is unable to extricate himself. Then, they turn the screws until the person yields and gives in to pressure.'

'Another trend that's come up fast these days,' said Devashish, 'is that of sending inappropriate messages to people. Modern technology plays a bigger role in this than it should.'

'One's personal life is one's own, I guess, but one is obliged to observe some degree of sanctity in professional life at least. Any wayward behaviour is indeed inexcusable.'

'I wonder,' said Manreet, 'what might be the psychological compulsions—apart from the lure of a luxury-filled life—that compel people to throw all caution to the wind and indulge themselves.'

'Maybe, only a psychologist can answer that!' smiled Nagpal.

'Are the reasons too hard for us to understand?' Shubhojit smiled. 'At times, we reel under the pressure and that too from all sides so that one wants and needs a quick getaway, even if temporary. The office atmosphere can be stifling; the wife difficult, the children irritating and demanding, the relatives persistent with their never-ending list of needs, and indignant if they are not satisfied. Everything and everybody gets on your nerves and you just want to throw it all up and give in to temptation.'

'Yes!' said Devashish. 'All you want to do is, cry out, "Fuck you all!"'

'You are right,' said Nagpal, 'and when you don't get relief from your own support system, you are automatically pushed towards external elements.'

'Let me share with you an incident from my youth,' said Shubhojit. 'My wife and I were on a holiday and were travelling by road. We had made arrangements for staying at a guesthouse, where I met an acquaintance who was working in the private sector and was also staying there. I thought he too had come with his family. But he introduced a pretty young lady to us, saying that he was on an official visit and was accompanied by his PRO. Well, they stayed in the same room and, the next morning, I overheard him talking in a very jovial mood to his children and wife over the phone, with the said PRO standing by his side.'

'Well, we come back to square one!' They all smiled.

'There are many such incidents and, as a society, we are at a crossroads. What we may see as immoral, is not so for the younger generation. All the same, it tarnishes the image and undermines the ethos of the service in public perception. Something needs to be done on a priority basis to save Sardar Patel's steel frame from becoming flimsy and irreparable,' said Manreet.

'You know,' said Shubhojit, 'when we are feeling low or depressed, we fail to communicate and share our thoughts with each other. We try to run away from our problems, and look for immediate diversions instead of facing them. If only we could talk to each other, just talk and talk...' Shubhojit let out a deep sigh.

'Or—how much I wish for this—if our own families could be as indulgent towards us, as we have been to them all our lives,' said Nagpal.

'I don't know why, but there comes a stage when we cannot make them understand our point and they refuse to budge,' said Devashish.

'It is only then that the real problem—the inability to understand each other's point of view—surfaces, and one is left all alone to fight one's demons,' said Shubhojit.

'We all have the same problems but we do not discuss them even among ourselves,' said Manreet.

'Why the bloody hell do we have to maintain a facade before outsiders as well as among ourselves?' Nagpal was furious.

'Well, the stress of our official life takes a huge toll on our personal lives and we pay a heavy price for it. People who indulge in heavy spending or philandering think that they are doing it discreetly. That none would know about it, little realizing that these matters are broadcast from the rooftops and are known to the whole world. One has to realize that the day one joins the civil service, one's privacy becomes highly restricted,' said Shubhojit.

'Still, we wouldn't exchange our profession or our lives for anything else,' all agreed. 'It's been a fascinating experience in many ways.'

Bahadur came out to invite them downstairs for breakfast. They decided to have it outside in the veranda. The sun beckoned as warmly as the hot aloo paranthas, which they loaded with dollops of home-made butter, the besan ka halwa and cups of foaming milky coffee. All the discussion was forgotten in the togetherness of the moment. They decided to postpone to another time the probing of their consciences. The steaming-hot breakfast needed their immediate and full attention!

7

YASHODHRA LEANED back in her study chair, absorbed in thinking of her last meeting with Shubhojit. Manidhar, her husband, was out of the country on a business trip and she had a lot of time on her hands. Although she had tried to adjust herself to her new surroundings and to the new man in her life, she could not rid herself completely of memories of her past life. They came back to her, again and again—even though it was close to about three years since they parted ways. After all, they related to a considerable part of her life and it had not been easy for her to move on. How could she erase the memorable years of her youth with just one stroke of the pen? Shubhojit had been her first love and he was still an integral part of her life in the form of their children. Yes, Neelakshi and Hemant were as much his children as hers and there was an inseparable bond between them.

Could it be that there was something still alive between her and Shubhojit? Yashodhra meditated over the possibility. Did he think about her as often as she did of him? Could they forget the years they had spent together and move towards a new future? Was it possible? Or, were they still in love with each other?'

Yashodhra could tell only about herself. If she were still in love with Shubhojit, that meant she did not care for Manidhar. But, if she now truly cared for Manidhar, she should have outgrown her feelings for Shubhojit. Either way, it was she who had borne the brunt from both sides. She was in a meditative mood.

Marriage to Manidhar had introduced her to a life of comfort and luxury, something she had always longed for. At first, she was overwhelmed by his wealth and the financial security their relationship had brought. It had opened her mind to the existence of various opportunities, unknown hitherto, in almost every walk of life. A whole lot of possibilities she had not dreamt of earlier. Away from a life of restrictions and inhibitions, the changed scenario had forced her to view life from a very different perspective.

'How strange and weird life can be!' thought Yashodhra with a sigh. 'One is always left yearning for something that is out of one's reach. When I was with Shubhojit, I dreamt of having a luxurious life, unlimited money, foreign trips, a cavalcade of expensive cars, family holidays etc. But there had been no possibility of all that! We led a circumspect life with a long list of dos and don'ts. Appearances had to be maintained at any cost, and expressing one's opinions was not encouraged. It was so stifling at times! There were only the right ways, the right means and methods for everything. The glamour was on the surface, hiding the reality beneath.

The ringing of her cell phone brought her back to the present. She decided to take the call. It was from Neelakshi.

'Mom!' she sounded upset.

'What is it, darling? Why do you sound so low?'

'Mom, Hemant is in trouble again. This time, he was involved in a brawl with his friends. They were all smoking pot and started arguing. Why don't you or Papa talk to him straight and hard?'

'Why didn't he ring me up?'

'For obvious reasons! Who wants to listen to a long lecture on the phone? Mom, he has gone absolutely astray. He needs direction. He is yet to come to terms with the idea of a broken home.'

'Your father is equally responsible!'

'Mom, let's not go through that whole drill again. Let's take care of Hemant's problems for now. The rest can wait!' Neelakshi cut her short.

Yashodhra felt a tinge of remorse. Had she taken the right decision? Could they have done better? The children had been the innocent sufferers in the fight between her and Shubhojit. If only they had had a little more patience with each other, they could have stopped short of reaching the point of no return.

Hemraj, the domestic help, appeared at the door carrying a tray with tea and light snacks. She asked him to put it on the table and leave her alone for some time. She took a bite and poured herself some tea. She was almost sobbing. Everything was a reminder of her past life.

'Can I ever be free of the memories? No!' said her inner voice. 'It is the past that shapes the future. There can't be a future without the past!' Yashodhra again fell into a reverie.

Even now, the intimate moments spent with Shubhojit were as real to her as was Hemant and Neelakshi's wonderful childhood; full of fun, laughter and love. It was the closeness that had made those moments so special.

Then, where had things gone wrong? When had they started drifting apart? What circumstances and compulsions had led to it? Why couldn't they have buried their differences for the sake of the children, who were so dear to both of them?

Yashodhra's eyes filled with tears. She wanted to relive the days of her married life and cry her heart out over them so that she could grow out of the relationship that still disturbed her peace of mind. She and Shubhojit had become so engrossed in the commonality of daily life that they had allowed life to become mechanical and uninteresting. Routine had become a rut and degenerated gradually into becoming monotonous and exhausting.

Her mind went back to an incident, the kind that had become frequent in the latter years of their married life. Shubhojit was supposed to be back by 8 p.m. that evening. They had to attend a dinner at the Golf Club. Yashodhra was all set to go. She loved socializing and was looking forward to meeting with her friends. She had chosen her dress and accessories carefully and was looking her best. Suddenly, the phone rang. It was Shubhojit on the line.

'Yashodhra!'

There was an eerie silence. She knew what was coming.

'Darling! I may not be able to make it in time. A lot of urgent work has cropped up. I'll be working late in the office.'

'We can go a little late?' she suggested.

'Why don't you go by yourself? You are an independent woman with a lot of confidence,' coaxed Shubhojit.

'First of all, did you really want to go?' asked Yashodhra in an icy tone.

'Yashodhra, you know clubbing and parties are not my cup of tea. You know I don't enjoy them at all, I consider them an utter waste of time. I don't want to be a part of that motley crowd of people with whom I have nothing in common. I shall send the car. You go and represent me!'

Yashodhra's heart sank. It wouldn't be the first time she was going alone. She came from a cosmopolitan background and could be at ease in any company. That was not an issue.

But she was tired of going by herself to such occasions, and becoming the butt of snide remarks and facing people's subtle, meaningful glances.

'Not that I care, at all!' thought Yashodhra. She had quickly accepted that she would have to follow her pursuits on her own, but it had been a painful process and had resulted in frequent arguments between her and Shubhojit. She found herself standing alone in society as well as in life. Two decades of marriage had brought out the marked differences in their personalities. They had been ardent lovers in the past, complementing each other's differences but, gradually, cracks had started appearing in the relationship on account of Shubhojit's busy schedule and his indifference to Yashodhra's interests. His lack of interest in the children's lives had further aggravated the situation.

Yashodhra had become increasingly aware that his long tenure in the civil service had hardened certain traits in his character, of which she had become weary: his self-complacency; his sense of righteousness; his conviction of always being in the right; adhering to avoidable, mechanical details; stereotyped and clichéd responses; a stubborn disregard for changing norms and life. Above all, he had acquired a tendency to lose his temper if contradicted and he would go a long way to prove his point. He indulged in idealistic monologues in arguments and could be vehemently censorious of whatever didn't please him or did not suit his ideas.

Yashodhra had also become bored with Shubhojit's tendency to repeat stories of his past exploits in earlier postings and bragging about them: 'You know, when I was in...'

Officers, thought Yashodhra, often forget that others may not be as interested in listening to these tales as they themselves are in telling them. And Shubhojit was no exception. If only he had taken, in the studies or lives of their children, a fraction of the interest he took in his professional life, Hemant and Neelakshi would have done so much better!

'What could I do? I was like a single parent for them. I did my best. I looked after the children; helped them with their studies; tried to keep a good house; took care of all the relatives, friends and acquaintances who frequented our home, uninvited; tended to our ailing parents; managed my own career and its compulsions, while Sahib sat smug in his office, indifferent to all the problems at home.' Yashodhra was still trying to work out the reasons for her broken marriage.

'If he had been a sensitive man,' Yashodhra reasoned out in her mind, 'Shubhojit would have been more considerate of me and my needs. After all, what did I really want? Maybe a cup of coffee or perhaps a candle-light dinner once in a while, or just accompanying me at least occasionally to social functions. Family holidays would have gone a long way towards keeping the family together.' Yashodhra went on and on in her mind. 'Shubhojit did not mind chatting with his colleagues in office or entertaining them with a cup of tea or coffee, or listening patiently to their woeful tales or funny anecdotes, but...the wife was always taken for granted...'

And then, Manidhar had come into her life like a breath of fresh air and rescued her from her stagnant marriage. Yashodhra met him at a cocktail party which she was attending by herself, and she saw him looking at her admiringly, a drink in his hand. He was middle-aged, cut a smart figure and had an expressive, intelligent look on his face. He came towards her and asked whether he could keep her company. Yashodhra, wary at first, was impressed by his charm and lingered for a long while, listening to him. Manidhar was a glib talker and knew how to hold the attention of female listeners. Initially, the tag of being a senior officer's wife had made Yashodhra attractive to him. Also, being in the good books of a VIP's spouse was important for him. Their subsequent meetings made him aware of the emptiness in her life as a result of her husband's busy schedule.

Manidhar was single and a globetrotter. He brought with him a new and different approach to living. He loved the good things in life and lived each moment fully as if it might be the last. He wooed her diligently and consistently. He made her feel wanted. He made her laugh. His company made Yashodhra forget her problems and the sense of negativity that had invaded her mind. He enthralled her with accounts of the various foreign lands that he had visited. He filled her imagination with visions of a world that existed beyond the limited, constricted world of the civil service. He kindled the dormant longings and yearnings in her heart. She fell for his charms and he found a receptive companion in her. And their growing intimacy wrecked the bliss of Yashodhra and Shubhojit's marital life.

8

Hemant and his friends were taken to the police station, where the sub-inspector subjected them to several rounds of interrogation. The noise, the commotion and the chilling atmosphere had subdued their sense of complacency and, to some extent, they regretted their reckless behaviour. They were still hungover and a bit lethargic under the influence of the drugs. Despite the police intervention, they were not overtly worried or, perhaps, they were trying to put on a defiant attitude. The police officers were smart enough to guess that these were not ordinary street boys, behaving, as they were, like brats of the rich and powerful. Hemant was the quietest of them all and did not join in the uneasy bluster of the other boys.

All of them were waiting. The boys were waiting for their parents and guardians to get them out of this mess. The police officials were waiting for a signal to make the next move. Meanwhile, Somesh, one of the boys, gathered courage and said that they were hungry.

'Can you please get us something to eat and drink? It has been a long time. If you don't mind, please! We'll pay for it.'

'Is it your father's home, idiots? How can you order us about?' shouted a policeman.

'We are not giving you orders. We are just requesting some food and water,' said Somesh. 'Our parents will reach any time. Please, bear with us till then.'

The policeman was a bit pacified. Years of experience had given him a kind of understanding that made him judge culprits according to their body language and behaviour. He could see that the boys were far from being habitual offenders.

'Ok! Let me see what I can do for you!'

The boys had to wait for some more time before help could reach them and the process of getting them out of this trouble could get started. Shubhojit came to know about his son's plight from Yashodhra. She had not hesitated to ring him up and ask for help.

'Shubhojit,' said Yashodhra, 'Hemant is in police custody. Please arrange to get him out of there.'

'What has he done this time? Why didn't he ring me up himself?' asked Shubhojit.

'Well, I don't know why. The boys had been smoking and drinking and perhaps fought over some girl. They don't share such problems with their mothers. Hemant might like to talk with you, if you would care to listen!' said Yashodhra.

'I wish he would, but he harbours a grudge against me for something. He is never frank in his responses. And he is never in a mood to share anything with me.'

'Are you keeping regular touch with him? He is trying to find some meaning in life but seems to be groping in the dark. Shubhojit, please help him. My heart aches for him. He needs a mature friend to guide him,' Yashodhra was almost in tears.

'Well, certain things are best left unsaid until later. Hemant is not a kid anymore. He should be able to figure out things for himself. Besides, I don't have the time to carry children along, holding their hands.'

'You never had either the time or the inclination. That's why the children are in this state now.' Yashodhra was stung by the harshness of his tone. 'Don't you have some responsibility towards him as a father?'

'What about the mother?' Shubhojit did not mince his words. 'At least I didn't run away from reality and leave them in the lurch.'

Yashodhra felt like shouting at him. Why was it that whenever she tried to talk to Shubhojit, a sense of animosity overshadowed all the other feelings between them? Every conversation only served to widen the gulf between them. Any attempt to make him see sense fell on deaf ears. This was an old game between them. They excelled in blaming each other and this had been the root cause of their break-up.

'Will you just shut up for now and get Hemant out of the police station?' she cried. 'What kind of a father are you?' Yashodhra was unable to control herself and hung up.

Shubhojit felt exposed and vulnerable; helpless and anguished. Hemant, the son of a distinguished and decorated civil servant, was now in police custody and was, perhaps, being ill-treated by them. In spite of his embarrassment, Shubhojit talked to his counterparts in the police department.

'Have I failed in my duties as a father?' he wondered. 'Was Yashodhra right when she said so? Why has my son gone astray? Could such a situation be avoided if I had been a little more involved in the lives of my children? Where have I gone wrong? I had entrusted everything to Yashodhra; true, but I should have extended help when she was dealing with problems. I had been too engrossed in my work and totally negligent of my family duties. I took it for granted that nothing could go wrong in my family life. Immersed totally in my secure world of power and privileges, I had expected the tenor of my life to flow smoothly and without any obstacles. I took my family's loyalty for granted. But what I conveniently forgot was that they were all humans, and as susceptible to pressures and temptations as me in this murky world of flattery and arrogance.'

In hindsight, Shubhojit saw that he had erred, and erred grossly. If only he could go back in time…only once…if he could recapture those precious moments, he would not let them slip out of his fingers. He would not allow events to take the shape they have now, he would change their course with his involvement and ability to deal with a firm hand. He would win his children's confidence and put them on the right path. He had allowed things to go on till they got out of control. And in the process, he had also lost Yashodhra…his lovely wife who had tried to do her best but, then, decided to part from him almost on a rebound. Could he blame her? If only he had taken her frustrations and discontent a little more seriously, perhaps, they would still have been living together as a family. His family had borne the brunt of his indifference, had disintegrated and was paying for his mistakes. Could he still make amends, somehow?

Shubhojit reached the police station and he walked inside with an uneasy mind. He was in for a shock as he entered the room: Hemant was sitting like a casual offender along with the other boys. He looked all around: it was a dirty, untidy, squalid room. Fragments of paper and bidi ends were scattered all over the floor. Empty plastic water bottles and beer cans could be seen lying in the corners. One or two undusted pictures hung crookedly on the bare walls. The heat was almost unbearable: one of the two fans revolved slowly and lazily, the other was out of order. Under the fan was a shabby table behind which sat a policeman, questioning an offender who meekly stood on one side. A number of chairs were placed in front, for the public. Hemant and the other boys were sitting in these chairs and were being given a tough talk by another custodian of law.

For a moment or two, Shubhojit went unnoticed and unobserved. As soon as Shubhojit's presence became known to them, they rose to their feet. The Station House Officer (SHO) came forward and saluted Shubhojit.

'Sir, please, take a seat! What will you have, Sir, a cup of tea or a cold drink?'

'Thank you! I have come straight from my office and have to go back soon.' Shubhojit was calm and matter-of-fact.

'Sir, you could have spoken to us over the phone…given your directions. We were just waiting to hear from you, Sir!'

'Have you registered an FIR, and, if so, under which sections?'

'Not as yet, Sir! They have certainly committed an offence, but, taking cognizance of their age and inexperience, we decided first to have a word with you. We are yet to proceed with the official procedure. Whichever way you would like to have it, Sir!'

'Would it be possible for you to let them off with a verbal warning this time? I mean, if they promise to behave themselves in future and not take the law in their own hands. If you can, please give them one chance at my request.' Shubhojit found it hard to look straight into the eyes of the SHO.

Basically a kind man, the SHO understood Shubhojit's plight very well, and the embarrassment he might be undergoing on account of his son being in such an awkward situation.

'That shouldn't be a problem, Sir! We'll manage! Don't worry, Sir! It is not unusual among young boys. I am sure they will be more careful and discreet in future.' The SHO, too, avoided eye contact.

While matters were being settled, Shubhojit was taken aback to see Neelakshi barging in, dishevelled and out of breath. Knowing that her brother had been and was still in trouble, and then hearing that he was being held at the police station, she couldn't wait. She was clearly disturbed and made no efforts to conceal her emotions. Shubhojit felt rather uncomfortable as she came running up to Hemant and hugged him.

'What the hell happened to you, Hemant? Why have you got into this mess? It is okay to have fun with friends but this is a wrong place to end up in. Think of me, at least, if not about anything or anyone else!' Neelakshi was in tears.

Her agitation increased all the more when she saw her father standing there, his head bent low. She felt sorry for him. The two still shared a strong bond and she was pained for him.

'When did you come, Papa? Are things under control?' Neelakshi's tone was worried.

'I came a while ago. Yes! The SHO has been very considerate.'

They both looked at Hemant who stood biting his nails and staring at the floor to avoid looking at them. He put a trembling hand to his forehead in an attempt to hide his nervousness.

As they all got up to leave the police station, a small commotion outside drew their attention. Yashodhra, looking distraught and a bit hesitant, was making her way in. For the first time, Hemant looked up and felt greatly relieved. It suddenly occurred to Shubhojit that he had been waiting for his mother all the while.

'What a shame,' thought Shubhojit, 'for the whole family

to meet at a police station under these circumstances!'

Yashodhra sobbed aloud as she hugged Hemant and kissed his forehead, 'Oh, my darling son! What have you got into?'

Hemant put his head on her shoulders and tried to control himself. He wanted to cry but was restrained by the awkwardness of the moment.

'I am sorry, Mom! You will never again be distressed on my account. There can't be a worse sight for a boy than to see his mother and sister in a police station because of him!' Hemant was overwhelmed.

'No concern for the father?' asked Shubhojit.

'We can talk about it later, perhaps,' answered Hemant.

'Sir! Would you like to have a cup of tea?' asked the SHO.

'Thank you so much for your help. It is time for us to go home!' Shubhojit shook hands with the SHO.

They all came out, at a loss as to the next step to be taken. The other boys walked away after thanking Shubhojit for his timely help and the once-happy family stood wondering about their course of action.

'Where do we go from here, Mom, Papa? Which home?' asked Neelakshi and Hemant.

Yashodhra stood motionless, eyes full of tears, while Shubhojit's face bore a blank and stoic expression. They were fiercely independent, all four of them. In the good old days, their friends would often joke about them that they were four separate individuals yoked together as a family.

Shubhojit looked at Yashodhra and then addressed his children: 'How about all of us meeting tomorrow for lunch and talking things out? Could you also join in, Yashodhra?'

'Yes, why not? Where shall we meet?'

'At the Gymkhana at noon. Let us spend some time

together.' Shubhojit hugged his children and offered to drop them back at their maternal grandparents' house.

'Let me do that, thanks,' said Yashodhra and hustled them away quickly.

Shubhojit walked towards his car, looked back at them, got in, took a deep breath and went his way.

9

Shubhojit's sense of propriety and dignity was badly hurt by the incident. It was hard for him to put it behind him. He probed deeper into existing doubts, into questions that lay unanswered at the back of his mind. His family life was in a mess; his children were rudderless and at a crossroads. If he didn't exercise restraint and caution at this stage, the consequences could be disastrous for them. Could he still intervene and control the downward slide of the family? What if all this had been an administrative problem? Would he still have been so lax and indifferent? Was there still a chance that he could at least steer their lives and put them back on the right track? He had made up his mind. And he still had time to mend matters.

Under no circumstances would he give up or allow his children to mess up their lives. He would deal firmly with them and take charge of their careers. Hemant was the first priority. He would be going back to the final year of his law school in a couple of weeks. He would have a heart-to-heart talk with him and make him see sense. He had heard from other sources that many such instances took place in law schools, where consumption of liquor and drugs was rampant. The daily routine was so packed and the academic grind so gruelling that some of the students took recourse to these substances without bothering about the consequences.

'Youth,' thought Shubhojit, 'knows no reason, only impulse!

That is where, perhaps, parents' role starts!'

Shubhojit remembered Yashodhra often telling him in the past that Hemant seemed to be straying away. But he had ignored her pleadings, citing as reason the normal growing-up process of boys. He had not cared to cross-check or confront Hemant. He had avoided visiting his son in the institution with the excuse of not wanting him to put on false airs about his father's status. Nor had he talked to his teachers over the phone. He had chosen to remain in the cushioned atmosphere of his own professional life.

They met at the Gymkhana the next day. Shubhojit had taken the afternoon off and meant to have an intimate talk with Hemant and Neelakshi. He saw them coming in together as he sat quietly at a table, waiting...waiting for people who had once been a family, not too long ago.

'How ironic!' The idea flashed through his mind. 'The situation has taken a full U-turn! Earlier, they all waited for me...day after day, for years on end and I never bothered much about it. Now, I sit here, waiting for them, in an attempt to put back on track my derailed family life.'

'Hi, Papa! How are you?' asked Neelakshi while Hemant greeted him more quietly. Mom said she would be a little late but she would definitely join us for lunch!'

'That's all right!' said Shubhojit, thinking that he would have some time alone with the children.

'How are your studies going, Hemant?'

'All right, I think!' Hemant was still in a sullen mood.

'What would you like to do with your life? You are in the final year of your course. It should be ending soon. Have you thought about it, Hemant?'

'I really don't know. I haven't made up my mind. I shall

have several options. Recruitment teams from the private sector will be visiting our campus shortly. If we come up to their standards, they might enlist us and offer jobs.'

'What about other avenues?'

'A career in law is another option. One needs to practise with a good, leading lawyer or law firm to gain experience.'

'What about the judicial service exams? Do you have any inclination towards those?' suggested Neelakshi.

'They are certainly worth a try!' Hemant was gradually coming out of his cocoon.

'Hemant, my dear son!' said Shubhojit. 'Where do you see yourself five years from now?'

Shubhojit's earnest question took Hemant by surprise and he looked straight at his father for the first time since they had met. Neelakshi, too, was taken aback by the force behind the question! Hot snacks were served. Shubhojit had taken care to order what the children liked the most: paneer tikka, spring rolls, potato wedges and manchurian vegetables along with mocktails. These provided enough diversion and allowed the question to seep in. Shubhojit decided to have a light-hearted dig at Hemant.

'Would you like to have some beer, Hemant?

Hemant was startled, but only for a moment. 'No, Papa, I'm fine!'

'I can keep you company, son. There is no harm in having some. Everything is fine in moderation. As long as one does not allow temptations to get the better of oneself.'

'I know what you are hinting at, Papa. There's no need to go about it in a roundabout way. We can talk straight.'

'Right, my boy! See, at your age, almost every boy indulges in these things: liquor, drugs, smoking etc. These excite the senses and young boys like to have a go at it. We all have had our share of such adventures. That's why I never tried to regulate your life as much as I should have, thinking that you would soon grow out of it. One has to know one's limits, one should not risk one's reputation or put one's life at stake.'

'Tell me, Papa. Why did you behave badly with my mother? Why couldn't you both sort out your differences? Why did you have to separate? Life's emotional ties can't be broken on account of trivial issues, such as that of incompatibility,' Hemant spoke in an anguished tone.

'Yes, Papa!' Neelakshi too voiced her unhappiness. 'If only you and Mom had been more patient and understanding of each other's problems a little longer, things wouldn't have turned out so badly. It has wrecked our lives! Did you ever think of us, Papa?'

Shubhojit was too pained to say anything. He hesitated to share the story of his marital life with his children. He did not want to expose himself to them. Neither did he want to enumerate the reasons for his and Yashodhra's break-up, nor add to what they already knew or had figured out for themselves.

There was silence for a few moments before Shubhojit said: 'Hemant, can you let bygones be bygones and take charge of your life? Getting embroiled in these things will lead you nowhere. You will spoil your health and lose a precious part of your life.'

Hemant sat still, eyes lowered, and refused to say anything.

'Hemant, dear, can you forgive me, forgive your father? I accept full responsibility for what has happened. I wish I could go back in time and force events to take a different turn. Son, I can't bear to see you like this, and, in this mood.

Don't throw away your life. It is valuable!' Shubhojit's eyes were moist. Hemant too was trying hard to control his feelings.

'Hemant, over-indulgence in drugs will ruin your health. Besides, combining them with liquor can prove fatal. Regarding any problems with girls, you better sort those out yourself,' Shubhojit patted his back. 'In case you like any one especially, you can introduce her to me.' Shubhojit tried to smile and put up a brave front.

'Papa, why don't you ask Neelakshi about her life? She too wastes her time on useless things. She is toying with dangerous ideas these days.'

'What dangerous ideas?'

'Not dangerous exactly in that sense! She wants to try her hand at modelling and hangs out with the wrong guys. She doesn't realize what a dirty world of exploitation this is. She will be like a lamb in a den of wolves!'

'You had better mind your own business first,' shouted Neelakshi. 'If you can do whatever you like, so can I. There can't be a gender discrimination in my case.'

'It is not a question of gender discrimination. You don't know, or perhaps, you do know that over-ambitious and pushy girls have to pay a price for their freedom. It is not a world where merit has any value. It is simply based on who can please whom and in what way. Are you ready to pay the price?'

Neelakshi kept quiet for a few moments before she could muster enough courage to say, 'I shall never compromise with my sense of dignity. But I want to make a mark in this profession. It fascinates me.'

'There are many ways to make your mark in life, Neelakshi,' said Shubhojit. 'You have neither knowledge nor experience of the ways of the world. You have led a very sheltered and privileged life at home. In this field, one has to either have a godfather or looks and talent.' Shubhojit was direct and firm.

'But, Papa, I am not a child anymore. I can figure out things on my own and take my decisions,' Neelakshi insisted.

'And, Neelakshi, you should be careful even with your dressing. You should remember that "less is more" doesn't apply to clothes. It applies only to make-up or accessories,' said Hemant.

'Oh, shut up, Hemant! Take care of your own life first.' Neelakshi banged her hand on the table.

While this heated discussion was going on, Yashodhra had been standing at a distance, unnoticed. She heard most of their conversation. In fact, she had not wanted to disturb them since, after a long time, they were opening their hearts to each other. Moments like these had been rare in their lives even when they were together as a family.

'Together as a family…' the phrase wrung Yashodhra's heart. A wave of sadness surged through her. She had a feeling of being left out in the cold while Shubhojit, Neelakshi and Hemant seemed to be still tied to each other in an unbreakable bond. It was she who had severed her ties with them by that one decision taken in a reckless and unstable mood. The abundant wealth and freedom she had found with Manidhar could not erase the memories of the sweet, honest and devoted moments they had once spent together…moments rooted in that middle-class morality which she had hated and from which she had fled.

Hemant was the first to see his mother and he immediately sprang to his feet. Yashodhra, dressed in a modern outfit and sporting a Gucci bag, slowly made her way to the table. Shubhojit got up and greeted her, pulling out a chair for her, while Neelakshi and Hemant hugged her hard and did not let go of her for a long time. No one spoke. There was no need for words. Each understood what was going on in the minds or hearts of the others. They were still a family, though physically separated.

'Shall we order lunch?' asked Shubhojit, looking at Yashodhra.

'Ah, yes! I am hungry!' she said.

'We, too, are famished!' Hemant and Neelakshi smiled for the first time.

Shubhojit felt at home for the moment.

10

ONE MORNING, on his return from a walk, almost an hour before his breakfast, Shubhojit decided to sit on the lawn for a while and relax. Ever since he had met with Yashodhra, Hemant and Neelakshi, he had been given to moods of introspection. He preferred to sit alone and think over issues that were disturbing him. Though they had discussed relevant matters without any inhibition, many issues were still left hanging in the air. They needed close monitoring on his part. Yashodhra, he knew, would always be there for her children, but she would have to do that from a distance, standing as if on the periphery.

The peaceful atmosphere lightened his mood a bit and he closed his eyes. He had been lacerating himself over his past indifference towards the needs of his family, which had led to this situation. As he looked back, he was irritated when he remembered the way his relatives and acquaintances had used him and his influence to further their own ends. The way they had thrown their weight around by boasting of their proximity to him. He had always tried to help others, in any which way he could, but the expectations of people had only increased along with his rank. The more he obliged, the more they expected of him. He had felt mentally exhausted and emotionally drained.

He ought to have put his foot down on many occasions, he thought. He opened his eyes. His phone was ringing. He picked it up and said, 'Hello!'

It was his father on the line. 'Were you sleeping, Shubhojit?'

'No, Babuji! I have just come back from my walk. How is your health? I hope mother is doing well.'

'Everything is fine. Some people are here with me and they want to talk to you. They need your help.'

'What do they want now? Their demands never seem to end. They don't understand that I, too, have my own limitations and compulsions.'

'At least listen to them! Your own village people have the first claim on you. You should do your best for them when they come with my recommendations.'

'Have I ever failed you, Babuji? What haven't I done for them? At times, they have convinced you with their inappropriate requests and made it embarrassing for me,' said Shubhojit.

'Shall I give the phone to one of them?'

'Yes, please!'

'Morning, Sir!' said a voice at the other end.

'What is it that you want? Tell me quickly. I am getting late for work.'

'Sir, we have a community-run girls' school in the village. You are aware of that.'

'Yes, what about it? It is running well, I assume.' Shubhojit was getting restless.

'Sir, we think that if the government could take over its running, it would be beneficial for all of us. We would not need to worry about finances and the teachers would become regular government employees with job security.'

'And spoil the school in the process? Do you realize that your children would be the biggest losers in the process?'

asked Shubhojit in a rather angry tone.

'But we find it extremely difficult to manage the school. We cannot engage new teachers and pay them reasonable salaries,' was the response from the other side.

'Increase the fees. You cannot run a school without some minimum resources,' said Shubhojit.

'Sir, if we increase the fees, at least half the parents would withdraw their daughters from the school,' argued the other side.

'I understand but it is not all that easy. There is a procedure for it. And these things take their own time,' said Shubhojit.

'Sir, we can, at least, start the process for that, if you would help us out, please.'

'You people should meet with the chief minister of your state for that. Let your group present him with a petition and impress upon him the logic of your demand.'

'Right, Sir! We will do that first and then get in touch with you again.'

Shubhojit hung up the phone. He reclined in his chair, folding his arms and gazing for a while at the greenery around him. He saw two persons opening the gate and waving at him as if to register their presence. Shubhojit recognized them. They were distant relatives from his mother's side. He knew why they had come.

'Good morning, Sir, we thought we'd catch you in the morning itself, so, we took the night train,' said the older one.

'What can I do for you? Have you had breakfast?'

'We had breakfast at the station. We have come to you again with the same request. You have to help us this time. We are in dire need!'

'See, there is a system for everything in the government.

Jobs are not to be found scattered on the road.'

'My son has applied for a police constable's job. He has already appeared in the written examination. Please help him clear the exam and then…make a strong recommendation to the DGP… Can I take it as done?'

'How can I do that? Sorry, but this will not be possible. Let your son clear the written examination on his own merit. If he is called for an interview, I shall try to put in a word for him,' said Shubhojit.

'Sir, everything is possible in our system. If only you will speak for him…'

'I told you earlier and I am telling you again now. There has to be some element of merit in a candidate before one can make a recommendation. Come to me at the right time,' repeated Shubhojit.

'Sir!' said the other one. 'My daughter-in-law has applied for a teaching job through the Short Service Commission. If you could talk to somebody and help her get the job, please?'

'Well, I don't know the chairman so well that I can make a request. Besides, it is extremely difficult these days for people to jump the queue.'

'I am sure, Sir, there must be a way out,' insisted the man.

Shubhojit was annoyed. 'Why don't you people try to understand when I tell you the truth? IAS officers are humans and also bound by a system. I don't have a magic wand which I can wave and get the desired results for all of you. I'll see what I can do! And now, I am getting late for office. Please excuse me but do have a cup of tea before you go,' said Shubhojit, and rose to go inside the house. He asked Bahadur to serve tea and biscuits to the visitors sitting outside on the lawn.

Shubhojit liked to get ready in a leisurely way. He was

running late today and had to rush through. He ate his breakfast quickly, gathered up his papers and ordered his file-box to be kept in the car. His mind was now fixed exclusively on the day's agenda. He had a few important meetings lined up and was not sure whether he would come home for lunch. Giving relevant instructions to Bahadur, he walked towards his car, throwing a glance in the direction of the lawn where he found the visitors still sitting; he got into the car and sped away. The privacy of the official vehicle, though only for a short while, always helped him streamline his thoughts and plan ahead. His face mirrored his thoughts: 'What a selfish world! No regard for another person's convenience or inclination. They think only about what suits them the best; they are vociferous in making their demands and they expect quick results from others.' Shubhojit was annoyed beyond words.

It took him only ten minutes to reach his office. Once inside, Shubhojit was a different person altogether. He liked nothing better than being at the helm of administrative affairs. His various postings in the government had given him enough opportunities to carry out his ideas. Challenging situations stimulated his mind and he took them up as personal problems. His PA, Jagjit, appeared with the day's schedule and gave him the relevant papers. He also told him that a large number of people were waiting outside to see him. Shubhojit looked at his watch. He had to leave for an important meeting in another ministry in about an hour. He told his PA that he should send them in to him one by one while he looked at the papers.

'Right, Sir,' said Jagjit and went out.

The door opened and four people appeared, jostling one another to be in front and catch Shubhojit's eye. Sweating profusely, they waited for Shubhojit to look at them and initiate a conversation.

'H'm!' said Shubhojit and asked them to sit. 'What brings you here?' he asked.

'Sir, we are from your sister's sasural. We have a request to make.'

'What is it, tell me.'

'We have to travel about twenty kilometres to reach the grain market to sell our crops. This route can be shortened to only eight kilometres if a new road is constructed by the Marketing Board. A survey has been conducted and the proposal has been under consideration for the last three or four years. However, it has been held up for one reason or another. Sir, please help us.'

'It doesn't come under my jurisdiction. You should go and meet with the concerned person,' said Shubhojit.

'Sir, nobody listens to the grievances of the common man. We have learnt that the chief administrator of the Marketing Board holds you in high esteem, and we feel that the construction will start the moment you speak to him,' they pleaded.

'Let me see! I'll try to speak to the right person. All right!' Shubhojit dismissed them quickly.

The door opened and the next lot came in quickly. Shubhojit nodded and motioned them to sit.

'Yes! Tell me quickly.'

'Sir, you have not recognized us, probably. We studied in the same school in the village.'

'Oh!' smiled Shubhojit. 'When was that?'

'A long time ago, a few decades, for sure. It seems like yesterday, though.' They all smiled widely.

'What brings you here, now?'

'We thought that if you could help us get the permit for a gas agency, it would ease our financial condition.'

'Have you applied for one?'

'No, we thought we would ask you first. Maybe if you could tell somebody to help us?'

Shubhojit was irritated. 'I don't control such permits. It is a different ministry. Apply for one and you should get your turn if you fulfil the eligibility criteria for it. I'll try and help you with the procedure.'

'You are in a high position today. Why don't you help your old classmates for old times' sake?'

'I have told you what I thought was right. Now, you would be wasting your time with me. Let me attend to my work,' said Shubhojit in an icy tone. The group went out with an air of resentment.

There was a buzz and Shubhojit picked up the phone. It was a call from the minister's office.

'Sir, the minister would like to speak to you. I am putting him on,' said the PA to the minister.

'Hello!' The minister was on the line.

'Yes, Sir!'

'Shubhojit! I have a few people from my constituency with me. They are very important to me. They have applied for allotment of industrial plots in various categories. I understand you still have influence with your colleague in charge of this corporation. I would appreciate if you could help.'

'Sir, send them over. Let me understand what they need and I shall do whatever is possible.'

The minister hung up the phone.

It was almost time for Shubhojit to go to the interministerial meeting. Leaving the necessary instructions with the PA, he asked for his car to be ready. He usually took the stairs instead of the elevator. As he was going down the steps, there was a beep on his cell phone. It was Sunil, his batchmate.

'Hi, Shubhojit, how are you?'

'Absolutely fine, Sunil,' said Shubhojit, 'going for a meeting just now. Anything important?'

'My cousin, who wants to set up an industrial unit in your home state, has applied for an industrial plot. Could you please help him?' asked Sunil.

'I suggest you mail the facts of his case to me and then let me see what can be done.'

'Sure, I will, and then we can catch up,' said Sunil and ended the call.

Shubhojit got into the car feeling a bit put-out. Since morning, he had been at the receiving end of the expectations of others in some way or the other. He wondered whether he should consider it a privilege or whether he was a victim of circumstances, or a plain milch cow.

Shubhojit could not decide for himself.

11

Manidhar had spent almost a fortnight touring Europe on his business trip. Yashodhra had accompanied him a couple of times earlier but, this time, she had decided to stay back. She just did not want to go. Her parents had been in delicate health for a while and she wanted to look after them. She wanted to be close at hand in case they needed her company or assistance. Besides, she was aware that her children were at a low phase in their lives and might need her support. She just had to be there for them whenever they sought her help or if they needed her at all. Post her separation from Shubhojit, certain awkwardness and a sense of distance had crept into her relationship with Hemant and Neelakshi and she felt herself alienated from them. Although they carefully desisted from articulating it, they held her responsible for taking a detour from their lives.

Manidhar had returned two days ago and was still reeling under jetlag and exhaustion. He was always happy when travelling abroad and had come back with a bag full of expensive gifts for Yashodhra. He had missed her company; her grace, her charm, her smiling face as well as her ability to rise to any occasion. Her ability to make meticulous arrangements in almost everything had brought a great sense of balance into his life. He no longer craved for the unbridled freedom of his young days or the love for novelty that had accompanied it. He had lived the life of a high-flier for as long as he could remember: plenty of money, sex, the company of beautiful women, and a dabbling in power. These things had always fulfilled his desires and given him a lot of sensual pleasure, but his idea of a happy and meaningful life had undergone a change ever since he met Yashodhra. She had brought with her a cool sense of composure; a maturity that could be deemed reticence but it was a quality he admired in her. She was the epitome of all he wanted in life now and he was proud of her accomplishments. But it had also brought about a strange sense of insecurity in Manidhar: the fear of losing her to another man or falling in her esteem and losing her respect. He often wondered how Yashodhra kept herself busy in his absence. Periods of long separation from her made him jittery and uneasy. But his work required him to be away for about half a month at a time and Yashodhra could not always accompany him.

Manidhar was aware of Yashodhra's frequent meetings with her children. He knew that Hemant and Neelakshi had been having a rough time and that Yashodhra, as a mother, just could not ignore their emotional needs. Rather, he had always encouraged her to be in regular touch with them, but the suspicion of her being in touch with Shubhojit too lurked in his mind. However hard he tried, he could not ignore the fact that Shubhojit and Yashodhra had numerous chances, and reasons, for remaining in contact, many more than he could imagine. And this sometimes made him apprehensive of the possible consequences even though he was aware that Yashodhra had left Shubhojit of her own choice and without any pressure.

Manidhar vaguely touched upon the subject in the evening. They had chosen to stay at home and he found Yashodhra sitting in the living room, alternately leafing through a book and looking out through the French windows. She remained absorbed in her thoughts even as Manidhar moved about the room in silence. He sat down on the sofa facing Yashodhra. She moved her eyes to his face and smiled. Manidhar smiled back but she could see that his mind was occupied elsewhere. At times, she wished she could peep into Manidhar's mind. He was in the habit of withdrawing himself from the outside world and taking refuge in a world of his own thoughts. She hated such moments. It was not difficult for her to guess the nature of his thoughts; but she was never in a mood to entertain his ambivalent ideas as such, if any. Since marrying him, she had learnt not to give undue importance to his moods and fancies.

At last, Manidhar broke the silence. 'How are Hemant and Neelakshi?'

'Oh, they are doing fine now,' answered Yashodhra.

'I understand Hemant had some trouble during the last few days. Has he come out of it?' he asked.

'Oh, yes! Things are much better. He will be leaving for his law school soon.'

'I suppose you sorted things out when you met with them.'

'Yes, we did!' Yashodhra kept a straight face.

'Whom do you mean by "we"?' he asked.

'Shubhojit and I!'

'Where was the need to meet him?'

'He is their father. It is easier for him to manage things with his resources than it is for me. And then, why shouldn't he take care of his children?'

'There is no problem in him taking care of his children!'

'Then, what *is* the problem?' Yashodhra looked sharply at Manidhar, who remained quiet for a few moments. It gave him time to choose his words carefully before uttering them. 'I only wondered whether it was necessary for you to meet Shubhojit at all; you could have just talked to him on the phone.'

'What *is* your problem, Manidhar? Even if I met Shubhojit, it was absolutely necessary under the circumstances. Besides, the children were also there with us and certain things had to be discussed together.' Yashodhra tried hard to keep her temper.

'Let me make it clear to you, Yashodhra,' he said. 'I don't like you being so much in touch with your ex-husband.'

Yashodhra was stung. The tone of Manidhar's remark offended her. 'Look, Manidhar,' she said. 'I have a past and a long one. It is not within my ability to wipe it out entirely. You were aware of everything when you wooed me out of that relationship. You should not object now.'

'I am not objecting in that sense. I was just giving a suggestion.'

'I understand it very well, Manidhar. But what you need to understand is that Hemant and Neelakshi are still far from being settled. I do need to be in regular contact with them and, sometimes, that makes communication with Shubhojit necessary. I fail to understand why that makes you so uncomfortable.' Yashodhra was emphatic. 'A major part of my life was spent with Shubhojit and that can't be erased. We outgrew each other and decided to move on. And that, too, was more of my decision than his. You have no reason to feel jealous or be over-possessive.' Yashodhra made her point loud and clear.

Manidhar quickly turned his head away and said nothing, at first. He picked a book from the mantelpiece and turned its pages rapidly while Yashodhra sat silent and agitated.

'You still have a whole lot of influence with Shubhojit, I guess,' said Manidhar at last. 'It is quite natural. I know I shouldn't resent that. I know for sure if I ever needed his help in any of my official deals, you would not mind putting in a word for me too,' said Manidhar in a sarcastic tone.

Yashodhra found this highly offensive and decided not to take it lying down. 'Manidhar, you are being unfair to me when you say things like that. It is not a question of who has influence on whom. You would have understood all this much better if you had had children of your own. Let me make it clear to you today. I shall always be there for my children whenever they need me and if that makes communication with Shubhojit necessary, I shall not hesitate to do so.'

Manidhar threw the book down on the table and got up. Without looking at Yashodhra, he said, 'I am going to the club and would like to have dinner there. Would you care to come along?' He waited for a little while, giving her time to reply but Yashodhra simply shook her head and picked up her book again. Manidhar quickly walked out of the room, shutting the door a bit harder than usual.

Yashodhra continued to sit in her chair. The spat with Manidhar had shaken her out of her usual composure. She noticed that such quarrels between them were becoming frequent. It was more so whenever Manidhar returned from his business trips abroad. He always came back with a bagful of doubts which disturbed her. It had not been so in the beginning. There had seemed to be a perfect understanding between them. Gradually, whenever Yashodhra was unable to travel with him, a situation like this would come up, leaving both of them in a sulk for days on end. Yashodhra sat frowning for a long time.

Nothing seemed clear in her mind today; if at all there was anything, it was a feeling of regret and helplessness. She found herself at the receiving end from all sides. The thought of the future filled her with a dread she had not anticipated.

'Why is Manidhar jealous of Shubhojit now?' she wondered. 'Didn't I leave Shubhojit for him? What is the cause of his deep-rooted sense of insecurity? He had entered into this alliance with open eyes, knowing everything. There is nothing that I held back from him. He can accuse me of nothing and yet this ugly situation has arisen.'

Yashodhra considered her options. It was impossible for her to retrace her steps now, even if she wanted to. She could only look forward to dealing with similar situations with a positive mind, and avoiding circumstances that might lead to acrimony between her and Manidhar.

'I committed a blunder once,' thought Yashodhra, feeling a bit nostalgic. 'I cannot commit another one! I must do the best I can,' she resolved.

Having made up her mind, she got up and walked about aimlessly in the living room for some time. 'Why don't I get ready and go to the club too? Manidhar will be there already!' thought Yashodhra. 'Yes, that's what I think I should do.'

As Yashodhra was climbing the staircase to go get ready for the club, she received a call from Hemant.

'Mom! Where are you? What are you doing?'

'I am at home and doing nothing right now, Hemant. How are you? I hope everything is alright at your end.'

'Mom, Neelakshi and I are going out for a quiet dinner. I shall be leaving for my school soon. Let's meet before I go back. Please, Mom! Hope you are free?' pleaded Hemant.

'Of course, I am free, Hemant. Always for my children!

I would love to join you. Where are we meeting?' she asked.

'Don't worry, Mom! Just get ready. We shall come and pick you up. Mr Manidhar, too, is welcome if he is free!'

'No, he has gone to the club for a business meeting. But I am free and shall be there.'

'Wonderful, Mom! We are coming for you!' Hemant hung up the phone.

Yashodhra was happy; she looked forward to being with her children once again. Meeting Hemant and Neelakshi gave her immense pleasure, anytime, anywhere. There were certain things that could never change even with the passage of time. Motherhood was indeed bliss in a way nothing else could ever be. Hemant and Neelakshi came to pick her up in a matter of one hour. As they were in a hurry, she met them at the gate and got into the car.

'Where are we going, dear?' asked Yashodhra in an affectionate tone.

'Relax, Mom! It is a surprise!' laughed Neelakshi.

The car arrived at the India International Centre, their favourite hangout place. What was more surprising was that Shubhojit was waiting at the entrance to usher them in and that too, with a smile!

Yashodhra felt both happy and sad, once again!

12

Both Yashodhra and Manidhar reached home quite late in the evening. Manidhar was surprised that she had gone out, especially after the heated talk that had taken place between them. He had expected her to be at home, in a glum mood. On the contrary, she was unusually happy and positive. In an effort to make peace, he asked her casually, 'You have had a pleasant evening, I guess!'

'Ah, yes! Very much so!'

'Went out with friends?'

'No! Hemant and Neelakshi came over to pick me up. We had dinner at India International Centre. It's not long before Hemant will be going back to his school.'

'You never seem to have enough of them!'

'How can I? They are my children.'

'Was Shubhojit also there?'

'He joined us a little late. The children insisted that he should come for a while.'

'Yes, of course! No wonder the reunion has had such a good effect on you!'

Yashodhra could see the direction in which the conversation was heading.

'If you have nothing more to say, may I go to sleep now? I am too tired.'

'Sure! Sweet dreams!'

Manidhar shut the door and went to the living room to

watch television for a while. He also needed some time to think things over. 'I think Yashodhra is bent upon humiliating me and that too in full public view. Why can't she exercise more restraint?'

Yashodhra walked about their room a little, preparing to go to bed and thinking all the while. She was getting tired of Manidhar's subtle but direct snipes at her past life. 'How can he be so inconsiderate?' thought Yashodhra. 'There is no doubt that there is a big difference between our value systems, but a little sensitivity towards each other's problems would make for greater compatibility.' She switched off the light and tried to sleep.

Yashodhra cried for a long time that night, feeling utterly helpless after Manidhar left her and went to another room. She lay thinking about his inconsiderate remarks. She felt a little guilty too; not so much about a possible change of heart, but that it had been her sole decision to end the marriage, whose outcome she had not foreseen, and with which she would now have to deal. And, she tried to do so according to her own good sense and judgement: she tried to give Manidhar the benefit of doubt. After all, he had come back to her after a long trip, looking perhaps for a loving welcome and some good company. The fact that he had missed her was not lost upon her.

A cold war of sorts had erupted between Manidhar and Yashodhra after their short verbal exchange. The morning did not bring about softer feelings towards each other nor an inclination for a truce. They spent their day wearing a non-conciliatory attitude on their sleeve.

'He deserved a better welcome from me,' thought Yashodhra. 'After all, men are emotional, and will always be.

Manidhar is no exception. Indeed, he is more so, since he has a towering ego and the worldly comforts to go with it. His bruised ego needs to be pampered, if I know him at all.' Yashodhra smiled and tried to put the incident behind her.

Parliament was in session and Shubhojit was extremely busy. His day began early; he tried to stick to his routine morning walk and to eat a healthy diet. Ever since Yashodhra had gone from his life, he had tried to maintain his health through diet control, regular walks and a monthly visit to the family doctor. The nature of his job didn't make things easier for him.

Parliament session days almost doubled his routine work. Whenever questions regarding his department were lined up in the House, it required a lot of prior data collection and preparation of replies. The whole office worked non-stop and Shubhojit would invariably be the last one to leave. He would often get careless about his meals: instruct Bahadur to keep his food on the table in the hot case and call it a day. After coming back, he would generally pour himself a drink and eat whatever he could at that late hour.

The proceedings in both houses of Parliament could be interesting on certain occasions. Shubhojit loved to witness these in person or on television. Going to Parliament, especially on question days, had become almost routine for him and his colleagues. The great House, a relic of the colonial past, was now a symbol of Indian democracy.

Civil servants were expected to be present in person before the various Standing Committees related to Budget, Assurances, the PAC (Public Accounts Committee) and other committees. They had to brief the ministers for replies to questions, and to assist them during question hour in case unforeseen supplementary questions were raised. Generally, they had to be prepared to be pulled up by MPs as a collective group, or individually. Most times, the MPs, separately, would empathize with the officers. There were moments of fun, laughter, tension, sarcasm as well as drama that could surpass any other show in political or social circles. The Parliament was a meeting ground for politicians, ministers, civil servants and, above all, the media. Serious business was conducted here; laws debated and passed; policies made; deals struck; friendships made, alliances broken. These interactions with the Members of Parliament were always a learning experience, though they could often be exhausting and frustrating.

It was late evening when Shubhojit returned home on the penultimate day of the Budget Session. The day's business had come to an end and he felt a sense of release—a sensation he had not experienced for a long time. He moved his reclining chair out in the balcony and sat there looking at the trees. The evening breeze moved gently through the leaves and he enjoyed the cool air. Bahadur brought soup after a while and Shubhojit enjoyed it sip by sip, tasting the freshness of the home-grown tomatoes.

Darkness was spreading fast. He watched with delight the soft, twinkling lights coming on in his house as well as in the neighbourhood, but he felt a bit restless and uneasy. The doorbell rang and Bahadur came to inform him that Adishankar sahib had come to meet him. Shubhojit got up and went down to the drawing room.

Adishankar greeted him: 'How do you do, Sir? Sorry, I have come uninvited, but I was passing by and thought of taking a chance on meeting you.'

'You are most welcome, Adi! It is so very kind of you. It

is always a pleasure to meet you.'

'Sir, you look tired. Hope you are alright.'

Shubhojit smiled. 'Would you care for a drink?'

'Sir, I shall stay only for a while. It is getting late.'

Bahadur brought out glasses and Shubhojit opened the bottle and poured out two drinks.

'Here's to your health, Sir!' said Adishankar.

'And to your happiness!' returned Shubhojit.

They held the glasses in their hands and looked at each other. At times like these, they just talked to each other like good friends. The delicate difference in hierarchy was overlooked for the moment, and they felt free of the constricting shackles of official life.

'What's the matter, Sir? You look exhausted,' observed Adishankar again.

'I am feeling a bit low and drained out,' said Shubhojit, 'but I have no reason to feel so. Maybe, it's the heat!'

'It is not so hot as yet, Sir. The weather has been fine till now.'

Bahadur brought out snacks: steaming-hot momos and paneer tikka. Shubhojit poured another drink for Adishankar. He put down his own glass. His mind seemed to him to be in a whirl. The sudden incoherence of his thoughts was beginning to startle him. He seemed to be thinking and not thinking at the same time. He tried to sit at ease and pick up his glass. Adishankar was watching his face with concern.

'What is the matter, Sir?'

'I feel quite hot. Maybe it is the alcohol,' said Shubhojit. 'Look at the way I am perspiring.'

Adishankar looked at his pale, drawn face. Drops of sweat were trickling down Shubhojit's temples. He had put his left hand on his chest and was gasping for breath.

'Sir!' asked Adishankar. 'Are you all right?'

'Adi,' said Shubhojit in a faint voice, 'I would like to see a doctor. I think I need help.'

'Sure, Sir!'

Adishankar helped Shubhojit lie down on the *divan*. He hastened towards the kitchen to call Bahadur and frantically began to call up for medical help. He phoned the Secretary, Health, who happened to be Shubhojit's batchmate.

'Sir! Shubhojit Sir needs immediate medical assistance. I am taking him to AIIMS. Please send word to have everything ready before we reach there.'

'Don't worry, Adi! Everything will be lined up. Make sure you reach quickly. Don't waste a minute! What's wrong with him?' asked Yadvendra Singh.

'Sir, he is gasping for breath, sweating profusely and clutching his chest.'

'Hurry!'

'We are leaving right now,' said Adishankar as he helped Shubhojit get into the car. He told Bahadur to take care of the house. 'You can inform Hemant and Neelakshi.'

'What about the memsahib?' asked Bahadur.

'Leave that to the children, Bahadur.'

As the car picked up speed, Adishankar looked at Shubhojit. He was breathing very heavily. Adishankar took out an aspirin from the first-aid box which was lying in the dashboard and gave it to him. 'Take this, Sir! You will feel better.'

'I am all right,' said Shubhojit 'Thank you very much, Adi. I don't know what I would have done without you.'

'Sir, we are about to reach the hospital. Don't worry, you will be in safe hands.'

The driver tried to speed along the road, slowing occasionally due to the traffic. When they entered the premises of AIIMS, a team of doctors was waiting to receive them, fully equipped and ready to get into action.

13

Shubhojit, surrounded by nurses and doctors, was wheeled into the emergency ward. He was immediately put on the support system before the procedure of thorough check-ups began. He was wide awake and a bit rattled by the flurry of activity around him. There were different technicians, headed by a team of specialists, monitoring different parts of his body. The doctors tried to put him at ease by indulging in small talk with him.

'Would you like to have some brandy, Sir?'

'No, thanks! I was enjoying a drink with my friend moments before I was brought here.'

The doctor smiled. So did Shubhojit. The small exchange of words helped lighten the atmosphere.

'How often do you drink?' asked the doctor.

'Almost daily!'

'Is it a habit? Or is it to pass the time, Sir?'

'It gives relief from troublesome thoughts. It soothes both my mind and body.'

'You will have to be careful in future. Maybe even exercise restraint to an extent. Health is as important as life!' The doctor smiled.

'Yes, I know!' said Shubhojit.

The ECG reports were brought in. The senior doctors were studying them intently and talking in hushed tones. Shubhojit was quick to notice this.

'What's the matter, Doctor?'

'The reports are not entirely normal. They point to a small blockage at the end of an artery. There is nothing much to worry about, though. It will be taken care of, definitely. Let me talk to the person who accompanied you. Is he a friend or a relative?'

'A colleague and friend both!'

'There might be some formalities to be completed.'

'You mean papers to be signed etc?'

'Yes, I suppose so.'

'If I may sign on my own behalf, I'll do that!'

'That will be fine. Let me talk to your friend and take a call on the line of treatment. Meanwhile, you should rest.'

The doctor returned, accompanied by Adishankar. Hemant and Neelakshi both had arrived. Bahadur's panic call had unnerved them and they had hastened to the hospital. While in the car, they had informed Yashodhra who, they were sure, must be on her way. They rushed towards the doctor.

'I hope our father is all right, Doctor! What has happened to him?' asked Hemant.

'There isn't much damage done, luckily. He has suffered a mild heart attack.'

'Heart attack?' Their eyes were wide with disbelief. There was a moment's silence before Hemant said, 'Hope he'll be fine, Doctor! What is to be done now?'

'We are going in for angioplasty. We'll try to clear the blockage to an extent. If need be, we'll put in the stents too. It is a decision we'll take on the spot.'

'Is it serious, Doctor?' asked Neelakshi.

'No! He has been very lucky. A tiny blood clot travelled through the entire artery and settled at the end without causing much damage. It has blocked only a miniscule area. That's why he didn't suffer much pain and was conscious right through. Also, he arrived here well in time, almost immediately after experiencing unease. He will be fine!' The doctor assured them.

'Are there any papers to be signed?' asked Hemant.

'Don't worry, Hemant! We'll take care of all that,' said Adishankar.

It was only a matter of moments before Shubhojit was in the operation theatre and the medical procedure for angioplasty had begun. Hemant and Neelakshi were keeping their fingers crossed while Adishankar stayed around, lending them moral support. The unexpected turn of events had shaken their sense of security and made them jittery.

'If only Mom were here!' they said to each other. 'She would have put everything in order. Ever since she left home, our family and our lives have disintegrated... But she must be reaching soon. She cannot sit at ease after hearing this news.'

'Oh, Mom! Come quickly!' they prayed with heavy hearts.

'Hemant, do you believe in God?' asked Neelakshi.

'I don't know, really. Why do you ask?'

'I am sure God can't be so cruel to us. We can't lose both our parents.' Neelakshi wiped a tear that had trickled down.

Hemant put his arms around her and hugged her hard, 'Don't worry, Neelu! I'll always be there for you. God willing, Papa will be fine!'

'Hemant, you are going to behave yourself in future, please. You will give up all that rubbish, won't you? Life is too short to indulge in bad habits. You have to grow up, brother!' Neelakshi's words went straight to his heart.

'Neelu, things are going to be absolutely fine. Don't worry!'

Brother and sister sat outside the operation theatre, hand

in hand, a prayer on their lips. Adishankar's presence was a great support. He had cancelled his plans for the night to deal with the emergency. Whenever the door creaked or opened, Hemant's and Neelakshi's eyes turned in that direction. They were waiting for their mother to reach.

Yashodhra came at last, not alone but accompanied by Manidhar. The moment she entered the room, Hemant and Neelakshi ran up to her and sobbed uncontrollably. Tears ran down their cheeks as she hugged them and kissed them on their foreheads. It was a moment she had been dreading ever since she had got into the car: it was difficult for her to control her feelings. Tears welled up in her eyes as she looked at the distraught faces of her children. She herself was equally distressed. She was standing at a crossroads: her sense of loyalty pulled her towards Manidhar, her present husband, but her heart pulled her in the opposite direction, towards her ex-husband. She was reminded of her first passion and the happy times with Shubhojit and the children. Though she had made a physical break from her past life, she had not been able to erase her memories of the home she and Shubhojit had set up with so much love during their youth.

Hemant and Neelakshi greeted Manidhar. He tried to console them and inquired about Shubhojit. 'How is your father? Are they through with the procedure?'

'They have been in there for a while,' replied Neelakshi. 'I am sure they must be getting to the end of it by now.'

'Don't worry. He will be all right.'

'Have you eaten anything, Hemant, Neelu?' asked Yashodhra. 'How long have you been here?'

'Oh! We had finished dinner when Bahadur rang us up,' replied Hemant. 'We started immediately and rang you up after getting into the car.'

'Thanks, Adishankar!' Yashodhra looked at him gratefully. 'Your being with him at that critical moment was a real godsend and your help was so timely.'

'Well, God is kind, Ma'am. I was only the medium,' replied Adishankar.

It was close to an hour before the doctors came out and spoke about Shubhojit. 'He is doing well,' said the senior surgeon. 'The angioplasty has cleared almost the entire blockage. A teeny-weeny bit still remains but medicines will take care of that. There was no need to put in the stents. He has been extremely lucky. You can talk to him for a few moments and then he can rest. We shall keep him in the ICU for the night and monitor the recovery.'

'Thank God, and thank you, Doctor,' cried Neelakshi. 'A doctor is like God on earth at times like these! Thank you so much, indeed!'

The doctor smiled. 'He has to stay in the hospital for a few days at least. We shall take a decision regarding that in a day or so. Let's see how he progresses. Meanwhile, go and talk to him. He must be waiting.'

Shubhojit's eyes were closed when Yashodhra, Hemant, Neelakshi and Adishankar entered the room. Manidhar chose to remain outside and talk to the doctor instead. The small sounds of people moving about and their whispering woke up Shubhojit. He opened his eyes and saw his family together. Hemant and Neelakshi held his hands and caressed him gently. Adishankar was all attention while Yashodhra kept quiet and avoided his eyes. It was evident to all that she was trying to keep her feelings in check. Though separated, it was hurtful for her to see Shubhojit in this condition. She felt as if her soft feelings for him were surfacing. She wished to be useful to him. She wanted to take care of him, albeit as a friend.

'Life can be so uncertain and fragile,' she thought to herself. 'We spend most of our life grumbling and nourishing grudges against one another but life can come to an end in a minute.' Yashodhra was getting philosophical and teary-eyed: 'Why do things happen in life over which one has no control?' She knew she couldn't stay there for long. Manidhar was waiting outside for her to come out. She couldn't stay in the hospital for the night. 'Maybe, I could,' she reasoned in her own mind. 'Am I not an individual in my own right? I don't need to consult Manidhar on this, if I don't want to. I can certainly opt for helping my children look after their father. Why can't I? Manidhar will have to understand.'

Shubhojit, though drowsy, could easily read her thoughts. In order to pre-empt any such move on her part, he said to the doctor, 'I need to sleep. I am feeling tired. I can see all of them in the morning. They should all go home.'

'Good!' said the doctor. 'That is exactly what is required at the moment. Let's allow him to rest. The nurse will keep a watch over him during the night. You need not worry!'

He led all of them out of the room. Yashodhra looked back and saw Shubhojit lying alone and looking at them with a heavy heart. Their eyes met and a wave of pain crossed their faces. None wanted the other to understand each other's feelings and yet they understood, and understood very well.

Manidhar's keen gaze did not fail to notice the emotions Yashodhra was going through. He tried to understand the state of her mind but the process was agonizing for him. He had always felt that he was yet to win Yashodhra's heart fully.

'Why does Yashodhra linger so much over the past?

Hadn't she made her final decision some time ago?' thought Manidhar. 'Whenever I feel I am getting closer to establishing an emotional bond with her, something happens and I get thwarted. Why did Shubhojit have to fall sick? Oh, God! Help me handle this mess in a calm and mature manner.' Manidhar too prayed to God, though for different reasons.

Hemant and Neelakshi were still nervous and confused. Adishankar told them to go home and sleep. They could come to the hospital in the morning. Shubhojit would also be much better then and able to talk to them. But Hemant and Neelakshi would not hear of it. They wanted to be near their mother and would not leave her side.

'Mom, come with us for the night, you just can't leave us to ourselves. We are so frightened for Papa. Do come for our sake, if not for anything else,' they implored her again and again.

Yashodhra was in a dilemma. She looked at Manidhar who looked away with a sullen face. Adishankar tried to ease the situation: 'Why don't both of you come with me? I shall be coming to the hospital in the morning anyway.'

'Thanks, uncle! You have been very kind. Your quick action saved our father. Our grandparents must be waiting anxiously for us. We should be going home now. And it is time for you too to go and take some rest,' said Hemant.

Hemant and Neelakshi turned towards the door, hand in hand, when Yashodhra blurted out in a determined tone: 'Go ahead, children! I am coming with you.'

She then addressed directly for the first time: 'Manidhar, I hope you won't mind. I might stay for a couple of days. I hope you understand my decision.'

'Yes, Yashodhra! I understand you. Make your decision!'

'Don't be so sarcastic, Manidhar! It is an unusual situation.'

'Your decisions too have always been unusual, Yashodhra. No problem, go ahead with whatever you think is right.'

'Interpretation of situations is always a relative decision,' Yashodhra cut him short.

All four came out of the hospital and walked in their different directions.

14

Shubhojit looked around when he woke up the next morning. There was no one in the room, he was alone. The room was long, dark and cool. It did not smell like a hospital. He lay for a long time waiting for someone to come and attend to him. No one came. Perhaps no one expected him to be up so early. Shubhojit was feeling much better. His bed was comfortable and he had slept soundly through the night. He did not have any pain now, nor discomfort. He looked at the shuttered windows, through which sunlight was coming in. Outside, the morning seemed fresh and beautiful! It was a new day! Shubhojit thought about the events of the previous night. Everything had happened so suddenly that his mind had not yet fully grasped the situation. His mouth was dry and he wanted a sip of water and some human interaction. He pressed the bell at the side of the bed. A nurse appeared almost instantly. She might have been resting in the next room, thought Shubhojit.

'Good morning!' said the nurse cheerfully. 'How are you, Sir?'

'Very well. Thank you.'

'What can I do for you, Sir?'

'I am thirsty, I would like some water.'

'Would you also like to have some tea?'

'Yes, please!' answered Shubhojit.

She went out of the room and came back with a bottle of

water. She had also given instructions for tea, she said. She came over to the bed and helped him drink water. She took his temperature and checked his blood pressure. She changed the bottle of intravenous drip and adjusted the other equipment.

'How much is the blood pressure?' asked Shubhojit.

The nurse laughed. 'You are not supposed to know that.'

'How am I doing according to your reports, nurse? Can I know that at least?' Shubhojit smiled.

'Very well. Aren't you feeling better, Sir?'

'Ah, yes! I feel almost normal.'

The ward boy brought tea and some biscuits. The nurse poured out some, and helped him sit up in bed to have it. Shubhojit took a few sips of the tea, found it bitter and somewhat cold, and refused to have more. He told the nurse that he would like to sleep a little longer.

'The ward boy will bring your breakfast in an hour or so, Sir. Meanwhile, you should rest. The doctor will come on his rounds at that time. If you need me, just ring the bell.'

'I shall sleep for a little while more,' thought Shubhojit, 'before the visitors start coming.' His parents, sisters, Yashodhra, Hemant and Neelakshi would probably be on their way already. He also knew it was only a matter of time before the members of his family in the village also got news of his health and start to pour in. He wondered how many visitors he would be allowed to have in the hospital.

The room was still dark. The little interaction had tired him and he dozed off again. He slept soundly for some time, dreaming about the good old times when he was a child and living in his ancestral village, along with his grandparents, parents and the other members of the family.

The village used to be a cohesive unit in those days and

people lived like a community, sharing each other's griefs, concerns and happiness. It was strange that he remembered those things so vividly even in dreams. They were in his psyche and his dreams were invariably built around them. At times, when he woke up bleary-eyed, he found it hard to distinguish between dream and reality. He would often feel as if he had been on a visit to his village and was coming straight from there. It was only the physical presence of the objects in the room that would convince him that he had been dreaming. Whenever he had shared his dreams with Yashodhra, he remembered her saying, 'Can't you dream of better things, Shubhojit? You have lived that kind of life during your entire childhood; it is time for you to grow out of it now.' Shubhojit would just smile and say, 'You Delhiites! What do you know about the pleasures of the rural set-up and community life? It is a world by itself; self-sufficient, generous, compact and based on mutual trust and sharing.'

Yashodhra would retort, 'You know, there is a world beyond that world too.'

Shubhojit would say, 'But not necessarily a better one...'

'How do you know?' Yashodhra would insist.

'I know. Someday I shall go back to it. Wait and see.'

'Well, I am not coming along. You will go all by yourself.'

'I know that too! Yashodhra, there is a world beyond personal relationships too. One has to grow out of these bonds to acquire a broader perspective on life.'

'You mean to say your village community teaches you that?'

'Oh, yes. Very much so! There is nothing like a personal life in a village set-up,' said Shubhojit.

'How frightening and oppressive!'

'Not necessarily.' And Shubhojit and Yashodhra would go

on and on putting their arguments forward.

Shubhojit heard a buzzing sound and woke up in a sweat. He felt disoriented for a few moments before the reality of hospital dawned on him. He looked out through the window. It was a bright, sunny day and it brought a smile to his face. He heard someone approaching his room. It was the nurse and the ward boy with his breakfast. He put the tray on the bed-table and asked whether Shubhojit would like to have tea, coffee or milk.

'Coffee, please!' said Shubhojit. 'But it should be hot.'

'Have your breakfast, Sir,' said the nurse. 'Then I shall make your bed and freshen you up. You will feel better. I shall be back in about fifteen minutes.'

Shubhojit ate a toast with a thin scraping of butter and a boiled egg. The boy returned with a jug of coffee and placed it on the bed-table. It was piping hot, and Shubhojit enjoyed it, sipping it slowly. The boy came after a while and took the tray away. The nurse returned with clean sheets, soap water and a sponge. She made the bed and smoothed the sheet under him. Then, she sponged him. Shubhojit felt clean and rejuvenated. She said that she would change his clothes later when his family brought a change from home.

'Thank you so much, Sister,' said Shubhojit.

The nurse smiled, 'You are most welcome, Sir.'

Shubhojit felt relaxed and looked out of the window. He could see the tops of the trees and the dense branches. He enjoyed the twittering sound of the sparrows in the balcony. It was close to an hour before the senior doctor, accompanied by a group of juniors and interns, walked into the room. He patted Shubhojit's back and addressed him. 'How are you doing, Sir? Had a comfortable night?'

'Yes, Doctor! I feel fine, though a little weak. I had a sound sleep and woke up just a while ago. How long am I going to be here?'

'Let's monitor your medical reports today and we shall take a call in the evening.' The doctor smiled. 'Sir, you have a rare chance of enjoying idleness or even daydreaming.'

'You are right, Doctor. I shall certainly do that. Then, please send someone to keep me company.' Shubhojit returned a mischievous smile.

'We shall shift you to the private ward in the evening, Sir. You will have access to more facilities there. Somebody can stay with you for the night. Also, a few visitors will be allowed to meet you during the stipulated hours. You will feel much better.'

'Thank you very much, Doctor!' said Shubhojit.

As the doctor was about to leave along with his team, he noticed that the director of the Institute was entering the room to meet Shubhojit and inquire about his health.

'How is the patient doing, Doctor?' he asked.

'He is doing fine, Sir! There is absolutely no problem,' replied the doctor. 'We shall be keeping a close watch over him during the day. He will recover fast, hopefully. He may be here for a couple of days after which we shall allow him to go home.'

'Take good care of him, Doctor,' said the director. 'Besides being the colleague of a very close friend of mine, the Health Secretary is keeping a close watch on his well-being. Take no chances!'

'Don't worry, Sir,' assured the doctor.

Yashodhra, Hemant and Neelakshi came in the afternoon. They were still subdued by the previous night's happenings and were trying to give each other moral courage and support.

Shubhojit lay in bed and watched them. They shared a close bond with each other. Shubhojit felt reassured that, in times of adversity or need, they would always be together. There are certain relationships in life, thought Shubhojit, that defy physical distance, and this was one of them. The thought made Shubhojit happy and relieved; in any event, Yashodhra would always be there for them.

Hemant and Neelakshi sat by his side on the bed and looked at him affectionately. Yashodhra took a chair. After a while, she asked, 'How are you?'

'Better!' said Shubhojit.

'You will have to take a lot of care once you get home,' said Yashodhra, keeping an expressionless face.

'Don't worry. I shall be fine.'

'I'll be there to look after Papa,' said Neelakshi. 'Mom! You and Hemant need not worry. And Hemant still has a week before leaving for the law school; Papa will be fine by then.'

Shubhojit patted Neelakshi who had tears in her eyes. 'Your Nana and Nani are there with you, Neelu. They will be here before long. Besides, your Dadi, I know for sure, will come and stay with me for some time when I go home.'

'Isn't she too old, Papa? She herself might need to be taken care of.'

'Oh, we'll take care of each other and reminisce about old times.'

The door opened, and the ward boy entered with Shubhojit's lunch, which he kept on the bed-table.

'What about your lunch?' asked Shubhojit.

'Don't worry, Papa! There is a canteen outside; we shall go and eat something after you have had yours,' said Hemant.

Yashodhra put some palak-paneer and dal on a plate

along with a chapati, and handed it to Neelakshi to help her father. Hemant held the bowl of curds. Shubhojit ate slowly and looked at his family. It was like old times. He did not mind being unwell and in the hospital. He would not mind however long it took if only it would help keep all of them together. Hesitantly, he looked at Yashodhra. For the first time since their separation, he felt that she still cared for him in some distant corner of her heart. He was an old habit for her and even though old habits might be nagging, still, they died hard. The thought made Shubhojit smile. Yashodhra, who sat at the other end of the bed, could guess what was going on in Shubhojit's mind. She smiled too, though in a restrained manner. After the meal was over, he felt like taking a nap.

'I would like to sleep for an hour or so, Hemant. Why don't you all go and have lunch?' Shubhojit suggested.

'Very well, Papa! We'll do that,' said Neelakshi.

They came back after an hour. Shubhojit was still sleeping. He woke up in the evening when the doctor came on his round to check on Shubhojit's progress. He examined him thoroughly, studied the reports and told Shubhojit, 'We'll shift you to the private ward, Sir. Any one of your family members can stay for the night.'

'I'll stay with Papa,' said Hemant quickly.

Yashodhra and Neelakshi nodded, looked at each other and smiled. Hemant had grown up to his responsibilities in a matter of one day.

15

Shubhojit was in the hospital for the next three days. He recuperated quickly and was in a cheerful mood. His medical reports were almost normal and he longed to go home. There was only one reason he would have wanted to stay in the hospital for a few more days: Yashodhra came to see him every morning and stayed till the evening. He had never enjoyed her company so much when they were together: he never had time for such things then.

'What a fool I have been!' thought Shubhojit with a tinge of rege. This was a facet of her personality—the ability to provide companionship and enjoyment—that he had always taken for granted. If only he had been as considerate to her as she had been to the family all her life! 'Marriages can sometimes fall apart on account of small issues and bruised egos!' pondered Shubhojit. 'If only one could realize it while there was still time…'

Every day, he looked forward to Yashodhra's visit. Her presence and pleasant personality lit up every nook and corner of the sanitized but insipid hospital room. He had always loved the subtle fragrance that she used. He had been so familiar with it that it had become an integral part of him as well. He remembered—it was Estée Lauder's Pleasures… Her coming to the hospital brought back memories of the olden days. It was like courtship once again. And he loved every moment of it. That she too must be reciprocating at least in her innermost being, he was almost sure of. Her body language had been positive right from the moment she came to see him for the first time in the hospital.

For Hemant and Neelakshi, the hospital room had become home. It was ages since they had had their parents together under one roof, even though for a few hours only. Gone were the bitterness, the resentments, the feelings of frustration, the acrimony as well as the trauma of coming from a broken home. Negative feelings were replaced by a new surge of positivity and hope all around. Hemant and Neelakshi moved freely about the room the whole day, fussing over their father and taking care of his needs. Shubhojit greatly enjoyed the undivided, whole-hearted attention being showered upon him.

'Shubhojit,' said Yashodhra, 'I may not be able to stay till evening today. Manidhar is going to have a few friends over. I will be needed at home.'

'It is perfectly fine, Yashodhra,' said Shubhojit. 'As it is, you have done enough. I know I can't lay any claims on you now.' Shubhojit heaved a deep sigh and looked at Yashodhra. Her eyes reflected the same agony.

'I shall leave around noon.'

'Sure.'

The family usually sat together and followed their pursuits after the routine medical check-up formalities were through in the forenoon. Shubhojit liked to read the newspapers for a while and the children kept busy working on their laptops or talking to their friends on their cell phones. Yashodhra would sit in a chair and try to read a book. They often talked about general things too.

That day, Yashodhra was in a hurry. She hugged the

children, shook hands with Shubhojit and picked up her bag and was about to leave when she saw Shubhojit's mother and sister entering the room. Unable to react, Yashodhra stood nonplussed. The awkward moment was eased by the loud greetings of Hemant and Neelakshi who embraced their grandmother affectionately. She cast a glance towards Yashodhra and her face stiffened with indifference or contempt, nobody could tell. Yashodhra simply folded her hands in respect. Shubhojit's sister completely ignored Yashodhra.

Neelakshi was quick to come to her mother's rescue. 'Mom, aren't you getting late?'

'Oh, yes! I'll make a move.' Yashodhra walked towards the door, accompanied by Hemant and Neelakshi.

'I'll see you all tomorrow,' said Yashodhra and walked out quickly.

Shubhojit's mother was in her eighties; a frail woman of delicate health but sound structure. Her shoulders were a little hunched, maybe due to osteoporosis, and she walked with a stick. Her face was round and full, though wrinkled, and her look was keen and sharp. She wore a big star made of gold as a nose-pin and a cotton dupatta. The children helped her come near the bed. She stood near Shubhojit and caressed his head.

'What have you done to yourself, Shubho? Take care of your health, at least for my sake.' Her tone was reproachful.

'I am all right, Ma! Doctors are going to send me home soon.'

'It is me who should be lying in bed, not you. Look at me, hale and hearty!'

'Ma, you people lived in the village for the larger part

of your life. You led a tough but meaningful life; enjoyed good food, pure environment; simple living and hard work. People hadn't heard of words like tension or stress those days. They lived together, ate together, worked together, shared their concerns with one another, and had community development as their sole aim. The general atmosphere in the village was always one of happiness and cooperation. I can never forget those times, Ma.' Hemant and Neelakshi, who had been listening intently, looked at each other and smiled. They had been familiar with these kinds of outbursts of their father since their childhood.

'Get well soon, Shubho,' said his mother, 'and then visit your village for a few days. It's been a long time.'

'Yes, I shall, Ma. Definitely.'

Hemant and Neelakshi made their dadi and bua sit comfortably in the chairs. Hemant went out to get some tea and biscuits for them. Meena, Shubhojit's sister, started talking to Neelakshi.

'Has your mother been coming every day?' she asked.

'Yes, she has been,' replied Neelakshi.

'What business does she have with you all, now? Why does she come?'

'Well, she is our mother and our father is sick. She feels concerned.'

'Where was her concern when she left Shubhojit for that stinking rich son of a bitch?'

'Meena, please. Mind your language!' said Shubhojit.

'Bua,' said Neelakshi, 'my father is not well and he should not get excited. You need not say such things about my mother. Every single person in the world has his or her own compulsions, including you.'

'It is easy to find fault with others, Meena,' said Shubhojit. 'In any fight, both parties are to be blamed equally.'

'Forget the past, Shubhojit,' said his mother, 'take care of yourself and your children now. Both Hemant and Neelakshi are yet to be settled. They need you and your support.'

'Yes, Ma. Let me get over this health problem for now.'

They all chatted for a while, each taking care not to hurt the other. Shubhojit's health was the most important issue. He was the pivot around which their lives revolved. They had to be careful not to disturb him in any way. Meena had felt snubbed initially but she saw sense in what they said. She had always got along very well with Shubhojit. It had been as difficult for her to accept Yashodhra's separation from Shubhojit as it had been for him. Her sympathies had understandably been aligned more towards her brother.

Hemant returned with cups of coffee and packets of biscuits and chips. It was interesting for Hemant and Neelakshi to see how their grandmother dipped the biscuits into the cup of coffee and then put them into her mouth. She looked at the children and said, 'I am an old woman. I no longer have my original teeth and use a denture now. Your father, too, used to eat like this as a kid when he was in the village.' Hemant and Neelakshi smiled and the old woman laughed too. She was very fond of her grandchildren and doted on them.

'Dadima,' said Hemant, 'we know that you are a very strong woman. Whenever Papa told us stories about his childhood in the village, no account was ever complete without some reference to you.'

'Your father was always more attached to me than to his father who was hardly there at home when the children were growing up. Meena, on the other hand, was her father's pet.

But we three were very close. Those were happy days.'

'Dadima, you will come and stay with us for some time when Papa goes home, right?' asked Neelakshi. 'He will feel happy and we will feel relieved because he will listen to your instructions regarding his health. He will never disobey you.'

'Of course, I am coming to stay with my son till he gets absolutely fine and starts going to the office.'

Kamladevi, Shubhojit's mother, was thoroughly enjoying the chitchat with her grandchildren.

'Hey, hey...yay...yay!' shouted the children. 'Dadima will be coming home. Papa is going to have a nice time.' Shubhojit's smile was an acknowledgment of the arrangement.

Shubhojit's mother and sister returned home in the evening along with Neelakshi. Hemant had taken it upon himself to stay for the night in the hospital. He would take a break in the morning when Yashodhra and Neelakshi came to relieve him, then return by noon.

Shubhojit stayed in the hospital for another two days. The doctors were satisfied with his progress and were contemplating discharging him in the evening. Initially, he would have to take convalescent leave for at least a month, followed by a medical check-up at the end. If he wanted, he could work from home till the doctors declared him fit enough to attend office.

Shubhojit was discharged in the evening and he thanked and said goodbye to the hospital staff. Yashodhra and Neelakshi had put his stuff together and Hemant helped him sit in the wheelchair. The doctors had come to see him off and give him the necessary instructions: about medicines, precautions to be taken and health care.

'Sir, you are doing very well. We hope your stay here was comfortable. You have to be regular in taking your medicines as well as exercising diet control. We will call you for a check-up after a month, till then we recommend complete rest. Only the barest necessary movements are allowed for you, nothing else!'

'I shall keep your advice in mind and take all precautions,' said Shubhojit with folded hands. 'Doctors, I have been taken good care of and I am eternally grateful to you all. For me, this room has been my home in the hospital; it had all the advantages.' Shubhojit smiled and looked meaningfully at Yashodhra and the children.

The doctors patted Hemant and Neelakshi on the back and said, 'Take good care of your father!' They greeted Yashodhra with a polite nod.

The family came down in the elevator, with Hemant pushing Shubhojit in the wheelchair. Hemant and Neelakshi were in a cheerful mood, but Yashodhra had gone quiet. She was making an attempt to remain composed but was filled with a peculiar uncertainty. Shubhojit could understand her state of mind.

'Yashodhra!' he said, looking at her. 'I deeply appreciate your kindness in coming here all these days and lending a helping hand. Only you could have done it. I admire your grit and I hope Manidhar has taken it in the right spirit.'

'It is all right, Shubhojit,' said Yashodhra. 'I somehow felt duty-bound.'

'Duty-bound? Not heart-bound, Yashodhra? You are no longer bound by duty, not in the least bit.'

'I don't know why but I just felt I had to come. And I did.'

'Will you come again, Yashodhra?' Shubhojit asked earnestly.

'I don't know!'

'Why not?'

'How can I?'

'You will always be welcome. Remember that!'

'We must not say such things!'

'We must meet again. For old times' sake!'

'What is the use of all this talk now?'

'There is always a future! And the future is what we make of it.'

'Let me think it over!' smiled Yashodhra and walked away.

16

It was late in the evening by the time Shubhojit and the children reached home. They would stay with him overnight. Yashodhra had approved of this arrangement. Bahadur was in high spirits on account of his sahib returning home. He had tidied up the house and tried to make his homecoming as happy as possible. He walked about the house like a man in a great hurry, making arrangements and giving the necessary instructions to the other staff. He was happy to see Hemant and Neelakshi after a long time and made plans to cook their favourite food. He asked Neelakshi about what sahib would need to have for dinner. The soup was ready and he could make other things in a jiffy.

'Would khichdi be good for him,' he asked, 'along with steamed vegetables?'

'I think that would be just right for today, Bahadur.' Neelakshi was appreciative and nodded her head.

'What would you and Hemant baba like to have for dinner?'

'Whatever you can prepare, but something nice,' smiled Neelakshi.

'Paneer tikka, dal makhni, biryani and lachcha parantha?'

'Will you be able to make all this so quickly?'

'Half the things are ready,' said Bahadur. 'I just have to assemble them. I anticipated your coming, Didi!'

Neelakshi was thankful to Bahadur for being there for

her father. He was an old, faithful retainer who had been with them for the last two decades. His loyalty and devotion to the family had seen them through good times and bad. They could depend on him in every way. She felt reassured.

Hemant, meanwhile, was busy settling his father in his room and keeping his things handy for him. He shouldn't have to exert himself, he thought. He still had a few days left to go back to the law school and, meanwhile, he would help his father as much as he could. The incident had shaken him badly and he realized, for the first time in his life, the importance of parents in the lives of their children. The possibility of losing them had frightened him and toughened him so that he was taking things more seriously.

'I could have done much better all these years,' he thought, 'perhaps, I can still do so!' He made a resolve in his mind never again to make his parents feel ashamed of him or his behaviour. He dreaded the idea of ever having to live his life without their support and guidance. His father had been his role model before he separated from his mother.

'Perhaps they had their reasons,' thought Hemant with a cool mind. 'It was wrong on my part to have judged them. Maybe, I can make amends now. It is not too late. I shall try my best to make them feel proud of me.'

Hemant was making an effort to reason out in his mind the transitoriness of life and the futility of useless quarrels and ego hassles. Shubhojit lay on his bed and watched his son lost in his thoughts.

'What are you thinking, Hemant?' he asked in a soft tone.

Hemant came and sat on the bed beside his father. He leaned over and placed his head on Shubhojit's chest. Shubhojit was surprised and overwhelmed. He put his arms around his son, brought him closer and hugged him hard. Hemant tried to suppress a sob. Shubhojit understood and wouldn't let him go. He wanted his son to be done with it: this letting go of one's emotions when they become unbearable. It would do him good.

'You needn't worry, Hemant,' Shubhojit caressed him. 'I am not going anywhere. I am going to be perfectly fine and that's my promise to you.'

'Papa, I'll be serious about my studies now onwards. I shall give you no opportunity to feel ashamed of me in any way, ever. I shall also take care of Neelakshi, always,' Hemant wiped his tears, 'and that's *my* promise to you!'

Father and son talked to each other as man to man, for the first time, ever since they could remember. It had been long overdue. Shubhojit's illness had broken the wall between them and they were ready to take on life, hand in hand.

'Papa,' asked Hemant, 'is there still a possibility of my mother coming back?' He tried to avoid his glance.

Shubhojit turned Hemant's face towards him, looked him straight in the eye and said, 'Only if I have both my children along with me!'

'We were always here, Papa. Only you couldn't find us!'

'I know! I have paid a heavy price for it. Let me try again now!'

The next morning, Shubhojit woke up feeling quite refreshed. His room was on the first floor of the house and through the window he could see the new leaves on the jamun tree glistening in the rays of the morning sun. The row of fruit trees next to the outer boundary wall ran along the main road, where people could be seen going for their morning walks. It was getting warm and Shubhojit got up from his bed and came out on the balcony. The fresh breeze made him feel even better. He rang the bell and asked Bahadur to get him his morning tea along with the newspapers. He sat on the reclining chair and looked around. It was like sitting in a green valley; all he could see around was tall trees and dense shrubs and the chirping birds.

'How strange!' thought Shubhojit. 'I had forgotten that there was so much beauty around. When and why did I stop noticing it?' It is great to begin the day surrounded by the bounty of nature even for half an hour in the morning. It is like recharging one's soul in solitude and preparing oneself for the day ahead. The gruelling office work sucks the soul out of a man's body till nothing is left of him except an empty outer shell and a frozen mindset.'

He noticed a parrot flying past and finally settling on a guava tree. The slow breeze swayed the tree branches from side to side. The bird hopped from one branch to the other, perhaps deluded into thinking that it was swinging the branches. It pecked lightly at a fruit and left it half-eaten. The fruit fell to the ground. Shubhojit laughed aloud. 'The bounty of nature versus the compulsions of the workplace,' he thought.

'Office? Oh God!' The reality dawned on Shubhojit that he was on convalescent leave. He had been advised complete bed rest for at least one month. How would he pass the time? He wondered how much rest he would be able to take without getting bored. His mind and body were so attuned to office work that he would find it hard to adjust to any other routine.

'Perhaps God had wanted to give me a message; send me a warning signal that there was still time and that I should not take life for granted; that there were other things in life equally important and necessary; that it was folly to ignore them and waste them; to not enjoy the beauty of the passing moments and the relationships. Oh, God! I shall become a philosopher at this rate.' Shubhojit smiled at the thought.

He had enjoyed his tea and biscuits. But he was not done yet. He wanted some more. He was hungry. He was enjoying this idleness; the getting up late in the morning and not knowing what to do; having no agenda for the day or a regimented schedule. He pondered over the constraints of his job. It was a system where you could be accused of bias if you had an opinion of your own; where, following the orders of the regime often pitted you in conflict with your own conscience and you were left with no choice but to continue as a robot, without feelings, emotions, conscience or soul. The price one paid, thought Shubhojit, was heavy; one's entire life was spent compromising with one's moments of happiness and meeting with the obligations of relationships. One's personal life was sacrificed at the altar of duty and professional compulsions, and the gain was minimal.

'The gain?' The word, thought Shubhojit, mocked at him and his achievements. 'What had he gained in life?'

'The Prime Minister's Award and that too, twice!' said his alter ego. 'And the respect of the administrative clan.'

But for this, he had had to put everything on hold; his personal life was in a shambles; his family had suffered and scattered; his roots had been forgotten.

'Had it been worth it?' Shubhojit wondered.

His whole life lay open like a road map before him. He thought of the moments of challenges and excitement; of the satisfaction of having achieved difficult and almost impossible targets; of having rubbed shoulders with the most powerful people and the innovative intellectuals; of giving sleepless nights to the craftiest minds, bullies or habitual offenders and then, his own emergence as an indefatigable and towering personality among them all. Shubhojit laughed aloud.

He had not fared badly, but he could have done better; at least as far as his personal life was concerned. If only the family had figured somewhere on his priority list! In his quest for excellence, he had reversed the roles: office for home and home for office. He should have nurtured the two equally, but he had taken his family for granted and expected them to adjust to his priorities. They had done so and had continued doing so for more than two decades but then, eventually, they had cracked under the pressure, while he stood on the periphery of their lives, unmindful and unconcerned, like a spectator. He had left them in the lurch, to find their own vent routes and when they did so, he was devastated. Perhaps, he deserved it.

'Is it too late for me to make amends?' Shubhojit almost wished he could capture the past and rewrite it.

Bahadur came up to see whether Shubhojit needed anything else. Shubhojit asked for a piece of toast and some more tea. He also inquired whether the children had got up or were still sleeping.

'They are sleeping, Sahib,' said Bahadur, 'it is too early for them to get up. They also slept late, they were chatting till late at night.' He reappeared after a while with a plate of toasts and fresh tea. 'What should I make for breakfast, Sahib?'

'Something light, maybe poha for me. Ask the children when they get up. Give them whatever they want,' said Shubhojit.

'Sahib, don't worry about them. I know them very well. I shall prepare whatever they would like to have. Sahib, shall

I say something?'

'Yes, Bahadur! Sure.'

'Sahib, after a long time, the house seems like a home. It seems that happiness has returned to this home.'

Shubhojit smiled and picked up a newspaper.

'Sahib, do you need any help with your bath etc? Call me whenever you need me,' said Bahadur.

'Thank you, Bahadur! I think I shall manage. Do tell me when the children get up. We can all have breakfast together.'

'Right, Sahib!'

Bahadur went down in a hurry. He was a busy man in the mornings—he had so much to do. Shubhojit couldn't help smiling.

It was strange, but true. Shubhojit was enjoying himself. His mind was at peace and his heart seemed to be in its right place. He was going to make the most of this leisure time that had been forced upon him. He was expecting some guests from his village during the day. He needed to reconnect with his past life. He needed to go back to his roots and make himself secure in this world of mundane, fast-changing relationships. Perhaps this is what they mean when they say, 'Go back to the basics!' thought Shubhojit.

Here was an opportunity, a not-to-be-missed opportunity, to fill the empty spaces in his life. He knew his mother would come with the visitors and would like to stay on for a few days. But he would request her to stay longer. He would not let her go back so soon, so easily. He would make up for the lost time with her. 'A mother,' smiled Shubhojit, 'is the only person in the world before whom one doesn't need to put on any special behaviour or pretence. One can be absolutely genuine with her, unmindful of one's shortcomings.'

The door opened and Bahadur came in again. 'Sahib, breakfast is ready and so are the children.'

'Send them up, Bahadur, and bring the breakfast too!' Shubhojit was eager and ready to reconnect; and with all!

17

It was around noon when Shubhojit's mother arrived, along with a few relatives from their village. They were all much concerned about Shubhojit's health, except Kamladevi herself who had visited him in the hospital and knew that he was on the road to recovery. He just needed rest and somebody to look after his needs—physical and emotional.

'Son,' said an elderly relative, almost his father's age, 'don't work so hard that you neglect your health and fall sick!'

'Yes,' said Shubhojit, restraining himself from getting into a discussion, 'I shall be careful in the future.'

'Have your meals at regular times,' said an old lady whom Shubhojit addressed as Tai. 'Skipping meals or having them at irregular times is harmful to the body.'

'Tai, don't you worry! I shall eat my food regularly now onwards,' smiled Shubhojit.

'Don't forget your medicines, beta. Take them also on time,' said another one.

'After you get well, come to the village and stay there for some time. The natural environment will heal you faster.'

'Don't worry about anything, Shubhojit,' was another's assurance, 'we shall make your stay comfortable.'

'That has never been an issue,' said Shubhojit. 'I grew up in the village and have no doubts about being comfortable there.'

Bahadur came with a tray of tea and snacks. Shubhojit told him they would help themselves with the tea, and asked him to prepare lunch for all.

The guests enjoyed the snacks, picked up their cups, poured tea into the saucers and drank it, making slurping noises. Shubhojit found the chewing and slurping sounds a bit annoying, but overlooked it because he knew their hearts were full of tender feelings for him. Their manners were rustic and unpolished, but honesty and integrity marked their character. The tea over, they put their legs up on the chairs and made themselves comfortable as if they were in their own homes. They were tired and wanted to rest. Shubhojit asked Hemant to take them to the guest room, where they could take a nap until lunch was ready. Shubhojit's mother, however, preferred to sit with him in his room and talk. They had a great many things to share but Shubhojit was in no hurry. His mother was here to stay, while the others would go back later in the evening.

'Shubhojit,' said his mother, 'you have been talking a lot. You must be tired. Why don't you lie down for some time while I catch up with Hemant and Neelakshi? And yes, remember to take your medicine.'

'Yes, Ma, I shall,' answered Shubhojit and stretched himself out on the bed.

The sound of the door opening about an hour later woke him up. It was Bahadur, who had come to check on Shubhojit and ask whether he needed anything. He asked about his mother and children.

'Sahib, they are sitting in the other room, talking and laughing.'

'Is lunch ready, Bahadur?' asked Shubhojit. 'How long will it take?'

'Just about half an hour more.'

'Serve it when it is ready, Bahadur, and then call everybody. Let me also know.'

'Yes, Sahib.'

Shubhojit took about half an hour to freshen up and get ready for the day. Lazing around too, he felt, should have its own rules whereby one did not forego having a bath or changing one's clothes. Ever since he had got up in the morning, he was in a good mood. He did not feel weak and thought of walking around a bit. Maybe he could go down for a while when lunch was ready, if his mother did not raise any objection. Or he could have it here in his room while the others had it in the dining room. He picked up a magazine from the side table and was flipping through it when he saw Bahadur coming up with a tray.

'Well,' smiled Shubhojit, 'it is obvious my mother is in charge of the household. No wonder Bahadur has brought up my lunch!'

It was almost evening when the guests decided to leave for home, which was about two hours' drive from this place.

'We shall reach before sunset, Shubhojit, and that is perfectly fine. It was very nice meeting you and our grandchildren also. Do take care of your health and get well soon,' said the eldest one.

They left with a hundred parting instructions and a lot of blessings. The day had almost come to an end and Shubhojit realized that he hadn't missed his office at all.

'Is it that I have had enough of office work? Have I reached saturation point? Am I completely burnt out? Surely, I couldn't be losing my drive and determination to face the coming challenges in my professional life. I still have a few more years to go before I can call it a day. Maybe I just needed a break.

And I hadn't opted for it myself, God had planned it for me this way. He has granted human beings the ability to adapt to diverse circumstances and then make the most of them,' thought Shubhojit as he lay reclined in the armchair.

Shubhojit had put his mother in the room next to his own. He enjoyed sitting out on the terrace in the mornings and evenings. After the guests left, he asked Bahadur to put an extra reclining chair there so that he could sit and talk with his mother.

'Bahadur,' said he, 'give us masala chai and, yes, put some extra tulsi and ginger in it. And help my mother sit in the chair.'

Bahadur helped the old lady settle in the chair and went to the kitchen to make the tea. He was also in a hurry to prepare the evening meal.

Kamladevi and Shubhojit sat on the terrace watching the sun go down in the west. It looked like a ball of molten fire. He saw the beauty of the throbbing, crimson sun and a wave of contentment washed over him. As it gradually sank through the blue sky, it left behind a soft, pink and orange hue. Kamladevi was mesmerized by the beautiful sight.

'Why don't we ever see the sun like this in our village?' she asked Shubhojit.

'Ma! The sun looks like this from anywhere. It is just that when you people sit together on your khats in the evening and indulge in community gossip or news, you don't have the time or the inclination to look at the sun and its beauty. It is a normal phenomenon for you all.'

'Beauty!' laughed Kamladevi. 'In village life, there is no concept of beauty, son. Everything is geared towards survival and convenience alone. Who has the time to think about beauty in that set-up? People living in towns and big cities think about these things. Villagers believe in the beauty of good actions and simple living.'

Shubhojit marvelled at the veracity of her statement. 'Rustic wisdom,' he thought, 'is based on practical experience acquired through a lifetime of struggle and hard work. And it has no parallel.'

Bahadur brought tea and biscuits. Two big mugs of masala chai made the way Kamladevi liked it: sweet, half-milk and half-water, boiled with spices. And a plateful of digestive biscuits, which she particularly liked. They were crisp and tasted very much like wheat. She would dip them in her tea and enjoy them.

Shubhojit was impressed by her streak of independence even at this age. Though he remembered his childhood days quite vividly, he wanted to go down memory lane with her. It would please her and also remind him of where he came from. It would also provide him with a much-needed diversion.

'Ma,' said Shubhojit, 'I know I was born in the village. I remember everything quite clearly even now. But somehow, I never cared to know about its history. Do you know when it came up and who the first inhabitants were?'

'Oh, Shubho! The history of the village comes down to us by word of mouth only. It is like an old myth. Our village, according to what we have been hearing from the elders through the years, is about 300 or 400 years old.'

'Ma, tell me all you know,' insisted Shubhojit.

'Why don't we call Hemant and Neelakshi also? Let them know about their forefathers and roots. It might seem like a fairy tale to them but the stories are based on facts and human wisdom. And these never change; these are universal in nature and character.'

'Yes, Ma, sure. It will do them good. What an excellent idea!'

Shubhojit rang the bell immediately and asked Bahadur to send Hemant and Neelakshi up to the balcony where they were sitting. They came after ten minutes, wondering why they had been summoned so late in the evening.

'What is it, Papa? I hope you are all right!'

'Of course, I am. Your grandmother wants to tell you the story of our village. Are you interested?'

'Certainly, Papa! We know nothing about our village or our ancestors.'

'Well, she is going to tell you all about it now.'

Kamladevi was immensely happy. She was enjoying the attention she was getting from her grandchildren. She had an opportunity to talk about things that were dear to her heart and that too with the people she loved the most in the world.

'Tell us, Dadima, all about our village!'

'Well, your village,' reminisced Kamladevi, 'dates back to almost 400 years.'

'Four hundred years?' Hemant and Neelakshi uttered in disbelief.

'Yes, that's the story which is told. Four brothers had come from an adjoining village almost 400 years ago to this place; they liked it and decided to settle down there.'

'How historic! Wow!' said Neelakshi.

'They named the village Bhainswal and divided it into four *paanas*.'

'Four what, Dadima?'

'Paana'

'In a village, the word paana refers to a section of population, divided into a number of households but descending from one common ancestor.'

'Oh, I see.'

'Each paana was named after one of the four brothers, who decided to take their lineage forward from there.'

'Dadima, do you know their names?'

'Yes, one was *Dungar* and his descendants came to be known as *Dungraan*. The second was *Bhoja* and his descendants are known as *Bhojaan*. The third was *Samta* and the paana named after him came to be known as *Samtaan*. And the last was *Mudal* and his descendants constitute the *Mudlaan* paana.

Bahadur came up to switch on the lights in the rooms and also ask about the evening meal.

'In about half an hour or so, Bahadur!' Shubhojit sent him away.

'Please go on, Dadima.' The children seemed greatly interested in the story.

'Each paana got further divided into *tholas* and, later, consisted of two or three tholas each.'

'What is a thola?'

'Thola refers to a clearly identifiable kutumb or a family, as it is known in our language,' Kamladevi explained.

'Papa!' said Neelakshi. 'This sounds like a political science lesson told in the form of a tale.'

'It is interesting to know,' said Shubhojit, 'how village society came up on its own and to know about its structure.'

'Village life was very simple initially,' said Kamladevi. 'Each paana consisted of many houses and they were all built in one row. People were engaged in agriculture and dairying to fulfil their needs for first, survival and then growth.'

'Papa,' said Hemant, 'Dadima's thoughts are so clear. Isn't it amazing?'

'Yes, my dear,' said Shubhojit, 'but this is just the beginning.'

'Why haven't ever we talked about all this before?' asked Neelakshi. 'It is so interesting. I can almost visualize our village and the way it has evolved through the ages. I can smell the earth. It is as if I were physically present there.'

'Who knows, Neelu,' said Hemant in a mischievous tone, 'you might have been present there in the form of a buffalo! You are eating all the time!'

'Shut up, Hemant!' Neelakshi shouted affectionately. 'Please continue, Dadima.'

'Tomorrow!' said Kamladevi; she had seen Bahadur coming up to inform them that dinner was ready.

18

Having their grandmother in the house and listening to her tales was like a picnic for the children. Kamladevi was an indulgent grandmother; she had met Hemant and Neelakshi after a long time since Yashodhra had gone away from Shubhojit's life. Even when Yashodhra had been living in the house, Kamladevi would get little time with the children. Her visits had not been frequent and whenever she visited them, the children had remained occupied in their own pursuits. Even Shubhojit was unable to spare much time for her on account of his busy schedule. It was Yashodhra who attended to her and gave her company.

For the first time, Kamladevi had the sole attention of Hemant, Neelakshi and Shubhojit. They all looked after each other; Shubhojit's illness had brought them together in one place and cemented their bond. The thread of lineage bound them and Shubhojit couldn't have been happier. Three generations of his family were under one roof and he loved to see the older and the younger ones getting along so well.

Hemant's law school was due to open soon but he had asked for an extension of two weeks on account of his father's illness. It had been granted, and Kamladevi and Neelakshi were ecstatic. They would all be together for a longer time; Shubhojit would be well cared for; grandmother and grandchildren would have an opportunity to interact further, and discuss the family history and the village set-up, something with which the children were absolutely unfamiliar. The atmosphere was congenial for good communication and it was leisure time for everybody. The family set up a routine. They would all meet at breakfast time; they would have a meal made to suit everybody's taste, relax and talk. The conversation was picked up from where it had stopped the previous evening.

'Dadima,' said Neelakshi, 'tell us more about the village.'

'About 70 per cent of the households, consisting of jats and brahmins,' said Kamladevi, 'owned all the land in the village. The next largest section was that of the scheduled castes, dominated by the chamars, who were the biggest agricultural labour force. At that time, the word chamar was not an insult nor was it ever used as a gaali as is done now. The rest of the population consisted of people practising other occupations.'

'What do you mean by other occupations, Dadima?' asked Hemant.

'Well, the households in the village were distinguished by their skills in different need-based occupations. These occupations were also identified with the castes of the people. For instance, there were five or six houses of baniyas, who met the villagers' needs for traded commodities and also acted as moneylenders. Three houses belonged to the *khaatis*, that is, carpenters, to take care of the woodwork, be it for joinery or household things or agricultural implements. Two or three houses were those of *lohars*, blacksmiths, who were engaged in manufacturing or sharpening agricultural implements.

'There were a few houses of *kumhars*, potters, who manufactured various sorts and sizes of earthen pots for household use. Then, there were two houses of *sunars*, that is, goldsmiths; two to three households of *telis* who were engaged in extracting oil and winnowing cotton; *jheevars* who did various odd jobs but were good at weaving baskets from branches of mulberry trees and who worked as *bharbhujas*—roasting of grains, particularly gram. There were a couple of houses of *baadis*, who were very good at acrobatics and gymnastics. Two families of refugees, who migrated from Pakistan, had also settled down in the village and soon emerged to set up all-purpose shops where you could buy different things, from vegetables and fruits to stationery and dry kirana provisions.

'An integral part of the village community were the people from the *nai* community, who were basically barbers, but their importance lay more in their role as marriage brokers and in attending to all the odd jobs during marriages. They liked to call themselves *thakars* just like the khaatis who liked to call themselves *jangra* brahmins.'

Shubhojit added, 'The barber was an expert in suggesting, making or spoiling matrimonial alliances across villages and helping them materialize, or break up. His expertise in matchmaking couldn't be questioned, nor his loyalty towards the family with which he was associated, and on whose behalf he would give out invitations. He enjoyed a special position in the family and was looked upon as a symbol of good social status.'

'Social status, Papa?' asked Neelakshi. 'What does that mean?'

'It meant that if a family changed its barber for any reason, it was considered nothing short of a social stigma. I still remember our barber, Munshi, who used to come and shave my grandfather. His son, Leelu, was a duffer and a laughing stock. Munshi was almost my grandfather's age and he could use only a machine for a close trimming of the hair.'

'Shubhojit, you still remember these things clearly,' said Kamladevi. 'It was considered the fashion in those days to get your hair cut with a pair of scissors. Munshi could not do that but his brother, Har Narayan, could. So, your father insisted on getting his hair cut by the latter. Your great-grandfather had to call Munshi first to get his nod before asking Har Narayan to do the chore for his great-grandson.'

'I can see,' said Hemant, 'that a barber was almost like a member of the family.'

'His importance increased manifold,' said Kamladevi, 'when the barat—marriage party—arrived from another village. He would entertain the groom's party and was always busy shaving the baratis or trimming their hair or helping groom them and freshen up. Invariably, the marriage party stayed in the village for at least two to three days and the barber would be in constant demand. He would strut around the village with an air of importance. Nobody dared mess with him!'

'Yes, I see, Dadima!' said Neelakshi. 'The village community was a self-contained, self-sufficient community, and didn't need outside help for anything. We have learnt about the barter system in the rural areas, which continued for a few years after Independence as well. But it is different hearing about it from a person who has lived through those times and knows personally about things as they were then.'

Kamladevi said, 'When I came to the village as a young bride about six decades ago, the barter system was used for certain commodities while cash was required for some others. These arrangements were at two levels: one, the relationship within the communities in the village, and second, procurement of the daily needs from vendors. Ours was a landowning family, and one family from each of these associated occupations was associated with us. This was known as the *jajmani* or *yajmani pratha*, according to which the landowning family was supposed to take care of the requirements of the associated family, be it the quota of grains for the year or fodder for their animals or any such things. Wages were rarely paid in cash till about the sixties. Mange was our *haali*, meaning ploughman, and he performed the arduous work, but his clout and status were in no way inferior to those of your great-grandfather. His daily meals in the field would consist of a lot of ghee and shakkar, that is, powdered jaggery, besides chapatis, dal and vegetables. As for the other associates, such as, the barber, the blacksmith, the carpenter, the sweepers etc, each of these families was associated with at least ten families of landowners and would get all their annual allowances in kind, more or less on a pro rata basis.'

'Does this not mean that they virtually worked for free?' asked Neelakshi. 'How could you always pay them in kind?'

'A relevant question, my dear!' Kamladevi agreed. 'Those customs and practices are beyond your imagination. They worked for us and we took care of their daily needs. It was an unwritten bond between the two sides. We provided them with their annual requirement of grains, and fodder for their animals; all that could be grown in the fields. Besides, cooked food would be given to the daily workers, for example, chapatis, buttermilk etc. For instance, the sweeper would be given four rotis and *chhach*, buttermilk, after he or she had finished the cleaning work. We didn't allow our utensils to come in contact with the ones in which they ate. Once, your father, when he was a small, mischievous child, intentionally touched my buttermilk container with that of our cleaning maid, and I had to part with my pot, which I gave to her.'

'Ok, Dadima, this was about the services. What about the procurement of provisions and how did the barter system operate?' asked Hemant.

'Well, things were not expensive then. Wheat cost almost twice as much as gram, at that time. So, anyone who needed wheat would exchange it for two times the quantity of gram. This system of exchange extended to pulses, vegetables and fruits. Our village had extensive orchards of good-quality mango, jamun, guava and *ber*. From the seventies onwards, all transactions, including wages, were done on a cash basis,' explained Kamladevi.

'As far as agriculturists were concerned,' said Shubhojit, 'the village set-up was like a cooperative society where everyone worked with mutual agreement.'

The conversation had gone on almost till noon. Shubhojit was showing signs of fatigue and wanted to rest for a while. Though he was enjoying the talk, his physical and mental abilities had suffered a setback owing to his illness. The children too needed a break.

Kamladevi grinned at the suggestion: 'I think I am the strongest of you all, even at this age.'

'Yes, Ma. You are. There is no doubt about that.'

'Dadima, you grew up in the pure and healthy environment of the village. In the cities, there are a number of problems, including that of pollution. Leading a life of stress is another deterrent to good health. Besides, you people consumed a natural diet that was rich in fibre and nutrients, and you also did a lot of hard labour. Yours was a tough generation!' laughed Hemant and Neelakshi.

'I can see that my grandchildren are getting well informed about such things. I think our informal talk is doing wonders to their general knowledge about the rural set-up, Shubhojit!' Kamladevi was visibly happy.

They decided to take a break for an hour and a half and then meet again for lunch. While the children got busy on their cell phones, Kamladevi went to her own room to have a leisurely cup of tea. She was not used to talking so much. Time passed in a jiffy and Bahadur was ready with the afternoon meal. He had prepared two kinds of cuisines: simple and light for Shubhojit and his mother; Chinese for Hemant and Neelakshi. They had set up an informal dining arrangement on the terrace outside Shubhojit's room. It was difficult for Shubhojit and his mother to come downstairs to the dining room for every meal. This arrangement, suggested by Neelakshi, suited everybody. Hemant offered to help Bahadur in bringing things up.

As Neelakshi and Hemant were setting the food on the table, the doorbell rang. Bahadur went down to open the door. He did not come up for the next five minutes or so.

'Bahadur, who is it? Bring the other things too.' Neelakshi called out.

Hemant was serving Kamladevi: yellow dal, a sabzi, curds, grated salad of cucumber and beetroot and a chapati.

Shubhojit preferred to serve himself. They were about to start eating when they heard someone coming up the stairs. It couldn't be Bahadur. At times like these, he was generally running up and down, bringing hot chapatis or a jug of water. The door opened and they all looked up.

It was Yashodhra! She had come up unannounced.

'Oh, Mom! How are you? Great to see you!' Hemant and Neelakshi almost ran to the door and hugged her tight.

'How are you, Shubhojit?' asked Yashodhra.

'What a pleasant surprise!' Shubhojit tried to appear calm, though it was evident to all that he was happy to see her. Kamladevi maintained an indifferent silence. Yashodhra came up to her and bent low to touch her feet.

Kamladevi's face remained hard though she tried to acknowledge her greeting with a reluctant nod. Neelakshi took it upon herself to ease the tense situation. She called out to Bahadur, 'Get one more plate for Mom, Bahadur.'

Hemant went inside to get a chair and placed it next to his own. They were going to make her feel comfortable and have a good meal together, despite their grandmother's reservations about Yashodhra's visit to their house. Kamladevi remained quiet throughout the meal, making it obvious that Yashodhra was no longer welcome to this house.

'She took a decision some time ago to desert Shubhojit and the children,' she thought, 'and she must stick to it now. She was not turned out of this house; she left it of her own accord. What business does she have to come back now? What does she want?'

Shubhojit inquired about Manidhar. 'Does he know that you are here?' He looked at Yashodhra.

'No! I don't have to take anybody's permission,' she replied, 'to do what I think is right. I just thought I would take a look at you and meet my children since they were here.'

'Papa! Can we eat in peace, please?' said Hemant.

Neelakshi got up and served everyone with a second helping. The food was delicious; they were hungry and also eager to please one another.

Kamladevi regained her composure and ate well. She had a healthy appetite even at this age. Shubhojit, the disaster management expert at office, was in command of the situation here as well. Hemant and Neelakshi had their family around them and couldn't be happier. They were trying their best to keep the atmosphere light and congenial. Bahadur came after a while to clear the table.

Kamladevi, looking at Yashodhra, asked her suddenly: 'Yashodhra! Are you happy?'

A look of pain crossed Yashodhra's face. She replied after a few moments, 'I don't know, Maji!'

'Then, why did you…?'

'Ma, please!' Shubhojit raised his voice a little, while Yashodhra covered her face with her hands to hide her tears.

19

Yashodhra was back in the fold, at least temporarily. As far as Shubhojit's mother was concerned, she felt that the old lady had thawed slightly. She had every right to be angry and to remain aloof, and that's how she had been when Yashodhra had walked in. But she seemed to have been softened a bit by her tears.

'The older generation,' thought Yashodhra, 'can be more forgiving, at times. Perhaps, age mellows them! Or maybe, the gradual loss of physical energy and strength impacts their emotional responses as well. They find it easier to take things in their own stride. They accept situations and circumstances without the acrimony of today's generation. They have seen more of life, and experience has taught them greater acceptance.'

Yashodhra herself was amazed at the ambivalent thoughts that were running through her mind. Was she thinking like a cynic or an eccentric? Why was it that one matured only after adverse experiences? Why did good sense prevail upon people, in many cases, only after they had dared to follow their own instincts and impulses? Yashodhra's heart was tossing and turning in a sea of emotions. But she felt waves of positivity coming from her former family. Hemant and Neelakshi, of course, had been in constant touch with her even after her separation from Shubhojit.

Shubhojit's illness had at least paved the way for a

normalization of her relations with him and his family. Yashodhra pondered the sanctity of human relations in situations like these which could test anybody's patience. She felt a peculiar yearning—she knew not for what—in Shubhojit's house. Yes, Shubhojit's house now…the home that had been hers some time ago.

'Shall I make a move, Neelakshi? I should be getting back.'

'Mom, lunch is just over. You can relax in our room for some time. There is so much to talk about,' implored Neelakshi.

'Yes please, Mom!' said Hemant. 'Stay with us for some time while Papa and Dadima take some rest. We'll have evening tea together on the terrace, watch the sunset and then I'll drop you home.'

'Oh, that will not be an issue,' said Yashodhra, 'I have the car and driver.'

'That's decided then, Yashodhra,' insisted Shubhojit.

Tea at five o'clock brought them all together on the terrace. The general atmosphere was a shade better and lighter than lunchtime.

'Isn't it a lovely evening, Mom?' said Neelakshi.

'Indeed!' answered Yashodhra. 'And the view from here is so good.'

'Somehow, I like the mornings better,' said Shubhojit, 'the air is much fresher and cleaner at that time. There is something magical about the early morning.'

'You hardly ever had time to enjoy the evenings.' The words escaped Yashodhra's lips.

Before Shubhojit could answer, Bahadur came up the stairs and started laying the table for tea and snacks. There was cold coffee and pakoras for the children; tea and idlis for Shubhojit and Kamladevi. Yashodhra could choose whatever she wanted.

They sat for a long time, sipping tea and enjoying the snacks, watching the sun set. The sky was beautiful, full of pure light and a dimming radiance in preparation for the night shadows to fall after a while. Yashodhra decided it was time for her to go back.

The day dawned next morning without any specific agenda for Shubhojit and his family. It was Kamladevi who looked forward the most to the morning routine. She was an early riser and by the time Shubhojit, Hemant and Neelakshi got up, she was through her morning routine. She would come out on the terrace, greet the morning sun with folded hands, water the tulsi plant and then sit for some time listening to the chirping of birds. It gave her immense pleasure. She would then go to her room, make her bed and have a bath. Feeling fresh and ready for the day, she waited for her family to join her for breakfast.

She loved the variety of the breakfast menu offered by Bahadur every day. Trained cook that he was, he had the experience and the expertise to serve the right dishes for the right people. Kamladevi looked forward to a different delicacy every day. While it was aloo parantha for all of them today, Shubhojit would have to make do with vegetable sandwiches and boiled sweet potato sprinkled with salt, black pepper and lime juice. There was tea, cold coffee and buttermilk to wash it all down with.

Kamladevi waited for breakfast to be over so that she could resume her tale of olden times. It filled her with a sense of nostalgia and satisfaction, as it gave her the feeling of having lived a full life.

'Dadima, tell us more. We are waiting for our session to begin.'

Kamladevi laughed at the mischievous glint in the eyes of her grandchildren. 'Yes, yes, with pleasure!' she said. 'Nobody likes to listen to the babbling of old people these days!'

'You may be old in body, Dadima, but you are young at heart!'

'Are you two making fun of me?'

'If you can digest aloo paranthas at this age and that too, two at one go, along with butter and buttermilk, Dadima, you are young even in body!' laughed Hemant and Neelakshi.

'Now, to get back to my story,' said Kamladevi. 'I shall tell you about two major activities in village life. The first was the harvesting season which involved the cutting of wheat when it was ripe in the fields.'

'Dadima, harvesting manually in such large fields must have been a very tedious and difficult task,' said Hemant.

'Yes, my dear! But it was a part of life and so we were all used to it. Our day would start early, very early, before the crack of dawn when we would go to our fields and do *laamni*...'

'Do what, Dadima?' asked Neelakshi.

'Do laamni. That's what the process of cropping the wheat is called in the local dialect. We would take our *daraanti*, that is, a sickle, and harvest the standing, ripened wheat that looked absolutely beautiful. The earth looked carpeted, as if with a golden tussar sheet, and it glowed all the more with the rays of the morning sun. It was a visual treat to watch the rising sun ushering in a new day of hope and fulfilment and it filled us with fresh energy. We cut large quantities of wheat every day, made bundles and stacked them together vertically. An expert was the one who could cut the stem closest to the earth so as to yield the maximum length and do it fast enough to complete the day's target. We left these stacks standing in the fields. We felt helpless, at times, about the unpredictable weather and prayed to God that it wouldn't rain.'

'We eat chapatis every day, but we never even dreamt that such a laborious process was involved in making the wheat flour that is available packaged in the shops,' said Neelakshi.

'The next step,' said Kamladevi, 'was what is known as threshing: loosening the grain or seeds from the husks and straw. The stacks of wheat, known as poolies, would be spread out in a circular fashion within a defined area. That done, the bullocks would be deployed to walk in circles around it, yoked to a *kolrahi*. That was a round agricultural implement made of stone, with cutters fixed around it at specified intervals. The pressure of the stone detached the grains from the 'head' of the plant, and the cutters chopped up the stems to be used as dry fodder for the animals. The whole thing would be lifted high in the air using a *jeli*. That was a wooden stick with four to eight iron teeth in the front. The air helped separate the grain from the chaff. This joint effort took at least two to three months, and all the families in the village would be involved in this.'

'Dadima,' asked Hemant, 'the grain would come out of the heads but it would still have to be separated. How was that done?'

'One man would put the threshed material into a *chhaaj*, and hand it to another person who stood on a high stool, and vigorously shook it so that the lighter chaff was blown away by the wind, while the heavier grains fell down. And that was the process of winnowing,' said Kamladevi.

'What is a chhaaj, Dadima?' asked Neelakshi.

'Well, I don't know any other word for it. It is a big rectangular basket made of dried grass or strips of cane. It is used only for this purpose. I will bring one when I come here next. Then, you can see,' said Kamladevi.

'It reminds me of Keats's *Ode to Autumn*, Hemant,' said Neelakshi, 'where he writes, "Whoever seeks thee abroad may find/Thee sitting careless on a granary floor/Thy hair soft-lifted by the winnowing wind." I can almost imagine it, Dadi describes it so perfectly.'

The grandmother gave a pleased smile and continued: 'Mechanization of agriculture completely changed everything. First, it was only the threshers; but now, wheat harvesting is largely done with combine harvesters. They are so called because, in one single process, they combine three separate operations—reaping, threshing and winnowing. Work that used to take us months can now be done in hours!'

'Dadima,' said Hemant, 'you people lived a very meaningful life unlike us. Ours is theoretical in nature in the sense that we do not connect with our surroundings at all. Yours was so action-oriented. There was another part of village life about which you wanted to talk?'

'First, I would like a cup of tea,' smiled Kamladevi.

After a break of about fifteen minutes, she started again. 'The second operation,' said Kamladevi, 'involved managing the crop of sugarcane with the onset of winter season in our part. Bajra and black gram, too, were winter crops. It was considered a taboo to uproot sugarcane before the festival of Diwali.'

'Why so, Dadima?'

'It was a myth or a tradition that has come down through the ages. It was a part of Diwali celebrations, a regular ceremony—taking five sugarcanes from the field on Diwali day—and it was usually referred to as *panchganda*.'

'Try to understand the rationale, Hemant,' Shubhojit interrupted. 'Diwali marks the beginning of the winter season, and sugarcane does not acquire sufficient sucrose till it has experienced the correct temperature. Hence, uprooting of sugarcane before Diwali was regarded as taboo. Similarly, a normal family consists of five persons. Hence, the concept of panchganda, meaning five gannas.'

'That is so interesting! Please go on, Dadima.'

'Since there were no sugar mills at that time, the only option was for four to five families to set up a *kolhu*, that is, a mill for crushing the sugarcane. One kolhu could process the sugarcane crop yield from about a hundred acre of land. Hence, it could never be an individual initiative, it had to be a joint venture; and this practice continued season after season, year after year.'

'But what did a kolhu *do*, Dadima?' asked Neelakshi.

'As I said, it was a mill, run by bullocks or, more often, by a camel, through which the sugarcane stalks were pushed.'

'Will you describe the entire process, please, Dadima?' asked Hemant.

'The end-to-end management of a sugarcane crop involved a few steps, starting with cutting the sugarcane, removing the top green portion—to be used as fodder—transporting the sugarcane from the field to the kolhu site, extracting the juice, boiling it on fire to make a concentrate, and then making gur, that is, jaggery, or shakkar, that is, brown sugar from it,' explained Kamladevi.

'The cutting of the sugarcane started very early in the morning. While a man kept cutting the stalks about four to five inches above the ground, the women would remove the dried-up leaves and cut the green portion off from the top. The sugarcane stalks were then tied up in bundles of about twenty to twenty-five each. This process was known as *chhol*. Some of the best sugarcane was reserved for home consumption.'

'But, Dadima, you say that sugarcane was cut four or five inches above the earth while the wheat stalks were cut as close to the earth as possible. Why was that?' Hemant was quick to ask.

'A very good question! You see, the sugarcane, once planted, stands there for three years. It is cut well above the ground to allow for the sprouting of new shoots, which are known as *mudha* (ratoon). They grow out to become the crop in the second and the third year,' explained Kamladevi, like a knowledgeable agriculturist.

'But, let us go back to the loading of the sugarcane bundles onto the bullock-cart and transporting them to the kolhu site. There was a taboo attached to that too,' she continued.

'Oh God! What was that, Dadima?' asked Neelakshi.

'No woman or girl was allowed to drive the bullock-cart which was called a *panjara*.'

'What was the logic behind it?'

'It was considered hard work. Besides, the bulls had to be kept under control. So, it evolved into a social taboo, perhaps over time,' smiled Kamladevi. 'Our social system was clearly defined at that time. The allocation of work was based on convenience and physical strength. We dared not defy it for fear of becoming social outcasts.'

'But when and how was jaggery made?' Neelakshi insisted on asking.

'Well, after the sugarcane was unloaded by the men, it was pushed through the kolhu, the extracted juice was collected in drum-like buckets and poured into the biggest of three containers. Next to it was a medium-sized and then a smaller one, all continuously heated over a common heat channel fuelled by bagasse.'

Neelakshi interrupted: 'What is bagasse?'

Kamladevi patiently explained, 'Bagasse is the dry pulpy residue left after the extraction of juice from sugarcane. It is used as fuel.'

'When will you come to the making of jaggery, Dadima?' asked the impatient Hemant.

She continued, 'Wait, son. I am taking you there. When the juice in the first container started to boil, it threw up the maximum impurities, almost like sludge, which had to be removed a number of times. These impurities came up easily with the use of a natural clearing agent made from a plant known as *sakulai*. When the juice was reduced to about half, it was transferred to the second container, and when it was reduced to almost one-fourth, it was transferred to the third container. When it became semi-liquid and brown in colour, it was transferred to a flat container, placed off-fire, and allowed to cool down a bit before one started making jaggery cakes. Warm, freshly made jaggery is a mouth-watering delicacy.'

'I see! Are these manual processes still in practice?' asked Hemant.

'No, not to the same extent,' replied Kamladevi. 'The Green Revolution brought mechanization in its wake and replaced a number of inefficient manual processes. The kolhu was largely replaced by sugar mills. Wherever it is still in operation, it is now an electrically or mechanically operated crusher with a much higher capacity. Besides, the educated, younger generations started looking for white-collar jobs in urban areas in preference to the hard life in the country. The old saying that "dur ke dhol suhavne" (the grass is always greener on the other side) proved true in our culture and set-up too. The people got more and more attracted to the glamour of the outside world, money, education and a desire for freedom. They started breaking away from their roots and adopted new ways in the name of modernity. They failed to appreciate that modernity does not have to mean total severance from your roots; it includes adaptation to changes wherever required. Don't you agree, children?'

'Yes, Dadima!' replied Neelakshi, 'Look at Papa! He was born in the village, spent his childhood there, went abroad for higher studies and became a part of the most élite service of our country. Yet, he kept intact his spiritual connection with his roots and never lost touch with the ground reality.'

'Yes, he still misses those carefree days of his past,' said Hemant, 'and all those traditions and rituals of a community set-up. He doesn't want to accept the difference between the personal and the public life. For him, each transcends the other. Isn't it so, Papa?'

'Yes, for me, the scent of the soil is still too strong and irresistible!' said Shubhojit in a sombre mood.

20

Shubhojit felt that he was being taken down the memory lane. In a way, his illness had turned into a boon. Whether it was a much-needed rest or a welcome respite, he was not sure. It had brought his family together in a manner which would not have been possible any other way. His children had never had the opportunity to understand him or his interests. His mother had never had a chance to talk so freely about her younger days and about something which would also interest her grandchildren. Shubhojit was very happy for her.

It had brought Yashodhra back into his life, though only on compassionate grounds. It had also succeeded in lessening the feelings of bitterness that had been simmering in the hearts of Yashodhra, Hemant and Neelakshi about him. Perhaps they would be able to understand him better now. Perhaps, he would also be in a better position to understand their concerns, their aspirations as well as grudges. For some time now, his relationship with his family had come asunder. But, he was beginning to see a silver lining to the clouds which had overshadowed his life.

The talks with his mother and the presence of Hemant and Neelakshi put Shubhojit into a retrospective mood. He seemed to be on a journey into his past. Picking up the thread of reminiscences, he asked his mother, 'Weren't many boys born in the *kunba* around the time I was born, Ma? I remember having many friends when I was a little boy.'

'Oh, yes! At least eight or nine boys were born within the family during that same year, with a gap of a month or two between the births. They were also given similar-sounding names: Rajinder, Birender, Surinder, Devinder, Ram Mehar etc,' laughed Kamladevi.

'Ma, I still remember those days very well; growing up with my playmates, sharing everything, laughing, crying, fighting and playing together.'

'Hemant,' said Shubhojit, 'you would laugh at the games we used to play. We would sit in the open air the whole day; make small mud drains with our hands and pee into them, imitating the irrigation of our fields. It would make us laugh hysterically. Even the elders would laugh along with us. We never had any inhibitions.'

'How weird!' Neelakshi wrinkled her nose.

'Yes, it does seem so now! Some of our other favourite games were: playing *ka-danka* on the low-branched jaal trees, gulli-danda or kanche, or pithoo—games you children have not even heard of. A field about two kilometres away would appear to be next door when rolling a hoop or a ring made of iron. These local games made us children street-smart and filled us with the spirit of comradeship as well as the determination to win. We thoroughly enjoyed those games,' smiled Shubhojit.

'Papa,' said Hemant, 'we too played gulli-danda when we were kids but Mom never allowed us to play kanche. She thought it was not such a good game.'

'The games that we village children played were largely convenience-based: we used what was readily available or what we could make of the material scattered around. I learnt swimming by hanging on to my buffalo's tail as it waded into a large village pond,' said Shubhojit.

Kamladevi had been listening intently and smiling to herself. 'Parents did not have much time to spare for the children,' she said. 'They had to be on their own, make up their own games, figure out things for themselves and help the elders when needed. This last one was their primary task.'

'Ma, you were always busy,' said Shubhojit. 'Somehow, the work did not seem to ever end for women in the village. Life is quite different in towns where one can set one's own routine. It was highly regimented in the village,' said Shubhojit. 'At least, as far as I remember! Wasn't it?'

'Yes!' said Kamladevi. 'But we enjoyed it also. We kept busy and hence, were physically fit. We used to be so engrossed in our work that we had no time to think at all. We never suffered from loneliness or depression as women in big cities do these days. We just did not have the time. Besides, we were always surrounded by people.'

'Dadima! Tell us about your morning routine. I would love to know what kept you so busy,' asked Neelakshi.

'Sure, my dear!' continued Kamladevi. 'We led a typical rustic life that could be representative of any village woman. We would get up very early in the morning, long before dawn, and start our work by preparing *saani*, that is, fodder for the cattle. It would be a mix of some dry stuff, some greens, oil cake and water. The green or dry jowar stalks had to be cut on the *gandasa*, a fodder-cutting machine, operated manually. That was done the previous evening and the men would also help. Then, the cattle and their areas had to be cleared of the previous night's dung and urine, before milking them. It required good training to milk cows or buffaloes and we were experts in that. The calves had to be fed first to make the buffaloes ready to be milked.'

'It must not have been easy, Dadima, though it sounds interesting.'

'It wasn't difficult. It was work that needed some experience and we had it in abundance. Your father milked our buffalo for four years every morning and evening while he was in college.'

'Wow, Papa! You did? What about the cooking, Dadima?'

'There were still two major tasks to be done in the morning,' said Kamladevi. 'They were the most important chores around which a village woman's life revolved in those days. The previous evening, milk would be set in a special earthen vessel, called *biloni*, for making curds. The next morning, churning the buttermilk for taking the butter out of it was the first activity. This process was called *bilona*, and took almost half an hour; the chhach was then poured out into another utensil for consumption by all persons, including the associate workers. Neelakshi, you might have seen this in movies sometimes. It was an excellent natural physical exercise for women, something that your gyms cannot provide. Holding the wooden batons in both hands and pulling to and fro the rope twisted around the *rayee* (churner rod) would press all the points of our palms and exercise our bodies.'

'Dadima,' said Neelakshi, 'I can see that it was perhaps the most natural form of acupressure, something we thought was a modern concept. This was an exercise of the shoulders, arms and the palms which, through pressure on the right points, would keep the body healthy and fit.'

'Which was the other important task, Dadima?' asked Hemant.

'Well, let me come to the most important and also the most arduous of all the work. This involved grinding the grains in a chakki,' said Kamladevi. 'I don't think you have ever seen it.

Simply put, a chakki comprises two heavy, round stones resting on a fulcrum in the centre. The lower stone is stationary, while the upper stone can be rotated, holding the wooden handle which is fixed at its edge. Adjustment of a spoke determines the gap between the two stones and the fineness of flour that you need. In the centre of the upper stone, there is a big hole, through which handfuls of wheat or gram or any other grain are dropped onto the lower stone, while grinding. Every day, the woman of the house had to grind the flour for the family's daily need as well as the grain-mix for the animals. It might sound simple but the heaviness of the stones made it a gruelling task. It was, in fact, an excellent exercise for a woman's body, right from the shoulders to the waist. It kept their muscles supple and strong. Women involved in this work would experience very little pain during childbirth.'

'Bravo! No wonder the village women come out as very strong characters in real life,' said Hemant. 'I guess it was totally a down-to-earth life where there was no room for any kind of artificiality. Hard labour toughened them up physically as well as emotionally to meet with any challenge in life.'

'I hope, Dadima,' said Neelakshi, 'the morning chores were over with these.'

'Oh, no, my dear,' said Kamladevi, 'all this had to be done by eight o'clock, by then it was time to gather the cow dung and pile it in a corner called *gitwara*.'

'What did you people do with that? The smell must have been awful!'

Kamladevi was amused by the spontaneity of the remark. She wasn't offended. It was the most natural question and needed to be answered.

'After the cow dung was brought and kept in the gitwara,

it was separated into two categories—pure cow dung and the mixed one.'

'Oh God! Yuck!' said Neelakshi while Hemant let out a low chuckle.

'What was next?'

'The pure cow dung,' smiled Kamladevi, 'was used to make cow-dung cakes or *upalas* which were used as cooking fuel for the household, for igniting the hookah.'

'What about the mixed variety?' Hemant laughed.

'That was put into a nearby pit, where it would turn into manure in due course of time and could be used in the fields whenever required.'

'We used to read in our history books,' said Neelakshi, 'that cattle were an integral part of village life. They were as important as human beings, perhaps more. Their usefulness extended even beyond their life. How true, Dadima!'

'Yes, children!' said Kamladevi. 'Those cow-dung cakes dried naturally in the sun, after which we collected them and piled them in stacks in the shape of a conical hut in an open space. This was again plastered with a cow-dung mix to protect it. This was known as a *bittora*.'

'Oh, I see,' said Hemant, 'now I remember. When Papa used to take us to the village when we were young, I used to see these small conical shapes in the middle of the fields and thought they were huts. I wondered how people could live in them. At times, I saw cow-dung cakes on the medians of the road. I often thought of asking about it; I just thought it was the garbage on the road.'

Kamladevi smiled and looked lovingly at her grandchildren. 'This whole exercise met with at least 50 per cent of the fuel requirement in a household. Chapatis used to be made on mud-chullahs, and wooden sticks, along with cow-dung cakes, were used as fuel.'

'Tell us about the hookah, please.'

'The hookah was an important pastime for the men. They would sit in groups in the evenings, chat, discuss politics or play cards, and use one common hookah. It was a symbol of community life.'

'Dadima,' said Neelakshi, 'I have seen a hookah. My mother had bought one from the emporium to use it as a decoration piece in the drawing room.'

Shubhojit and Kamladevi burst out laughing and patted Neelakshi affectionately. 'Have you had enough for the day?' she asked.

'Yes, Dadima! And now all of us are hungry. Shall I ask for lunch to be served?' asked Hemant.

The lunch, as always, was simple but delicious. There was light, healthy food for the older generation while the younger ones could have a feast. Hemant and Neelakshi had come to their own home after a long time and Bahadur took it upon himself to look after them generously just like their mother used to.

After lunch, Shubhojit and his mother went to their rooms to have a siesta. They both needed it: Kamladevi was an old woman and Shubhojit was recuperating from a life-threatening problem.

After the hearty meal, Hemant and Neelakshi wanted a break from the informative session and serious exchange of ideas. Hemant decided to catch up with old friends, go for a long drive and perhaps eat out at night. Neelakshi opted for a short nap and relaxation till the evening. An old friend and a classmate were visiting from the USA and wanted to meet with her over a cup of coffee. They would do so, along with some other old school friends who also happened to be in the city. It would be a chance to reminisce over the old times, the schooldays and the childhood days.

'Whenever one relaxes, one's mind goes delving back into the past. I wonder why,' thought Neelakshi. 'It is also strange that one wants to take refuge in happy memories and relive them. A journey into the past always brings a smile to the face, and when it is a collective effort, the recollections become all the more endearing.'

Neelakshi could see her own self and her friends in pigtails, going to school wearing a blue-and-white uniform and carrying heavy school bags. The image seemed so real even now.

21

The next morning started in the same manner. Shubhojit and Kamladevi sat chatting while waiting for the children. Their interactive sessions were eagerly looked forward to.

'The mutual sharing,' they wondered, 'was it a sweet recollection or a catharsis or both?' Shubhojit provided the link between the old times and the present moment. He connected the past and the present, and was also trying to connect to the future. Perhaps, that's how a legacy is taken forward, he imagined. The seed of the future lies in one's past and if it had been golden, its glow might be carried in some way into the future too.

Hemant and Neelakshi were a little late that day. Perhaps they had slept late. Kamladevi sat wondering whether the children had lost interest in her talks. But Shubhojit thought otherwise. He knew for sure that the longing to connect with their past had trickled down to his children as well.

Bahadur brought breakfast and said that Hemant and Neelakshi would be with them in a short while. They had got up late and were getting ready. Kamladevi had a look at the breakfast spread: vegetable uttapam for them and omelette with bread and butter for the children. There was also a basket of fresh fruit. Shubhojit peeled an apple and shared it with his mother. Fruits were best eaten on an empty stomach, a great way to start your day, he thought.

'Good morning, Dadima, Papa! How are you feeling?'

Hemant and Neelakshi came over and hugged them both.

'Let's have our breakfast quickly,' she told them, 'and then I shall continue with my story, whether you people like it or not. Now, since you have got me started on it, you must listen to all that I have to say.'

She picked up her plate and placed an uttapam on it. 'I don't know what this is but I like the food Bahadur makes.'

'Oh! Ma, this is like a chapati except that it is made of rice and urad dal. It is a typical South Indian dish and is very light on the stomach. Try it! I am sure you will like it,' said Shubhojit. He poured out some buttermilk for her.

'What a change from the office routine!' thought Shubhojit. 'Breakfast should never be a rush-rush affair. It should be eaten peacefully and at leisure, something which has been a luxury for me all my working life.'

Shubhojit was realizing for the first time how a change in one's lifestyle could result in an atmosphere of positivity and happiness.

'Dadima, yesterday you were telling us about the life of the village women. I would like to know more,' said Neelakshi.

'You told us about their tight morning schedule. Did they go to the fields after that? Did they have any moments of leisure and fun?' asked Hemant.

'Yes, of course, we did!' said Kamladevi. 'There were five wells in the village and women would fetch water twice a day from them. The mornings were always a hurried affair since there were a number of household chores to be completed. It was the evening time which every woman in the village looked forward to. We would dress up for the evening in our best attire: ghaghra-kurti and an embroidered odhni. We would make these at home and decorate them with gota, patti and sequins. In the evenings, dressed in a riot of colours, women, in groups or by themselves, would walk towards the wells with *do-ghars* or *toknis* on their heads.'

'With what on their heads?'

'Do-ghars and toknis! A do-ghar was two earthen pitchers stacked one upon the other, whereas a tokni was a pitcher made of brass or copper. Whether it was a tokni or an earthen pitcher, a woman would invariably be carrying a double stack on her head. It used to be quite a festive scene. You can well imagine, Neelakshi, a group of women walking in a file with pitchers on their heads. It was a time of fun, light-heartedness and laughter. They would share everything with each other: moments of thrill, romance, attraction, sorrow, grief, quarrels, jokes—anything and everything under the sun. They made up impromptu songs, in their own dialect and communicated with each other through them. They expressed all their emotions, ideas, thoughts, fantasies in these songs. These songs were the product of their fertile imagination which came out in full form during this time.' Kamladevi sounded both nostalgic and ecstatic.

'Did they fetch any water or not, Dadima?' Hemant laughed.

'Of course, they did and a few rounds each time, Hemant!' smiled Kamladevi. 'Have you ever seen water being fetched from a well? Perhaps you might have seen in the movies. This too was quite an exercise. A bucket, tied at the end of a long rope, would be lowered into the well, either over a pulley or directly and, after it was filled with water, the bucket had to be pulled up again. The women waited patiently for their turn, chatting, joking and telling stories. They even sang songs in the meanwhile. It was their meeting ground, where they could relax, and also use this as an opportunity to flaunt their new odhnis, accessories or jewellery. It was fun.'

'Were young girls too a part of this jamboree?' asked Hemant.

'Yes, very much so! They would accompany their mothers, aunts or bhabhis. It was a chance for them to get to know each other. The women had to make several trips to the well since a lot of water was required at home. Besides the domestic consumption, they needed it for their own bathing purposes. The women always took a bath in their homes while the men would bathe at the well or tube well, or in the pond.'

'The roles were clearly defined on a gender basis, Dadima!' Neelakshi said.

'Let me tell you something interesting, children. At times, the men used the women's trips to the well to meet their wives and talk to them,' laughed the grandmother.

'Did our grandfather too meet you like that?' teased Hemant.

'Many times! Almost every other day,' smiled Kamladevi. 'There is no privacy for a married couple at home in the village set-up. They had to meet stealthily most of the time.'

'What a pity!' exclaimed Neelakshi.

'Not at all, my dear!' smiled Kamladevi. In fact, it kept the romance alive. It was always an adventure. Secret meetings had their own charm and we loved our escapades. One is always attracted to whatever is forbidden, and the marriages lasted without many problems. Have you ever heard of divorces in villages? It is more of a modern-day, urban concept where too much familiarity leads to contempt. We were grateful for our few and far more soulful moments of bliss.' Kamladevi looked meaningfully at Shubhojit who did not miss what his mother was trying to drive home.

'Dadima, you are such a romantic at heart!' Hemant and Neelakshi laughed.

Lunch was a welcome break for all of them. Kamladevi looked forward to meal times and Shubhojit liked the idea of his mother eating in his house. He admired her spirit of adventure even in food.

'What do we have for lunch today, Bahadur?' asked Kamladevi when he came to serve the lunch. 'You are an excellent cook!'

Bahadur, pleased with the compliment, said, 'We have paneer bhurji, mixed dal and *ghia* kofta today. Also salad and raita along with green chutney.'

Kamladevi loved that. It reminded her of old days. 'Don't we have anything for dessert?' she asked.

Smiling, he said, 'Yes, Maji! Custard with fruits!'

Kamladevi had a hearty meal. She was hungry. She had never talked so much, and continuously. The food replenished her and she was ready to speak once again: 'You know, children,' she began, 'after we came back from the well, it was again a closed existence at home. The house would be literally divided into two sections in the evenings. While the men sat in the front portion called baithak, the women would be at the back of the house, preparing the evening meal as well as catering to the wants of the menfolk sitting in front.'

'What did the men do in the evenings?' asked Hemant.

'They sat in a circle around the smouldering hookah. They gossiped, related stories or played cards, and even discussed community activities and local politics. Some of them utilized this time in weaving jute ropes. Those were their moments of relaxation while the meal was being prepared. The youngest among them would keep the hookah alive and ensure that the fire remained available for lighting the *chilam*.'

'What's a chilam, Dadima?' Hemant asked.

'Chilam is that part of the hookah in which you keep the tobacco under a cover and put fire therein. The fire made from dried upalas is the most preferred as it burns the tobacco slowly,' said Kamladevi. 'There were two protocols that were strictly observed: the oldest among them sat at the head of the charpoy while the youngest sat at the foot. Secondly, passing around the hookah was always the responsibility of the youngest among them. These were signs of respect for the elders. Occasionally, somebody would also sing a *ragini* and entertain the others.'

'What is a ragini, Dadima?' asked Hemant.

'A ragini is a folk song. It could be either a stand-alone composition or part of the poetic folk-drama, called *swang* in the local dialect. These swangs were often based on folklore but some of them held deep knowledge and universal truths, based on the ancient scriptures, such as the vedas, puranas and upanishads. Men belonging to various theatre groups, wearing women's clothes, would enact them on stage. The great Pandit Lakhmi Chand, commonly known as Dada Lakhmi Chand, is credited with the authorship of a number of them. He was illiterate and fond of drinking, but used to consult a couple of pandits who would read out the scriptures to him. He would listen intently and then compose his folk songs and dramas. That's why his creations are a storehouse of rustic wisdom, myths and humorous anecdotes. The swangs offer a rare, in-depth experience of life and its tribulations, told through the medium of songs and dialogues. They are in local dialect and only those who have come from the village can appreciate them,' Kamladevi said in a nostalgic tone.

'I remember my grandfather, Ma!' said Shubhojit. 'He used to sit outside our haveli and make *rassi* from jute, called *baan*, and then weave it together to be used for making a cot, known as *palang*. A special tool was required for combing the jute strands and the woven material had to be thick and dense and waterproof. The people of adjoining villages swore by his skill, expertise and experience in ploughing the field, making ropes and weaving cots. But he was not outgoing, nor very articulate. The image that remains in my mind is that of a man working all by himself and always doing something useful. He was selective about the company he kept. I don't remember him indulging in gossip, ever. He was also a simple man, highly skilled but a man of few words. I held him in great esteem at that time and still continue to do so. He remained a source of inspiration for me. He was also a crusader for social issues.' Shubhojit too sounded quite nostalgic.

'Dadima,' said Hemant, 'I think my father takes after him. I am hearing all this about my great-grandfather for the first time and that too from my father, but I can see similar traits in their personalities.'

'Yes, I agree!' volunteered Neelakshi for Shubhojit. 'Papa has never been outgoing nor has he ever flaunted his status or the authority that he holds, or ever gossiped. He has always taken on concerns that touch the lives of common people. His thought-process and decisions have always focused on the public good.'

'He has never bothered about his personal life, either,' continued Hemant. 'Often to the detriment of his personal interests. I always used to wonder from where he had picked up his ideologies. He has been a solitary and silent worker.

He doesn't care about public acclaim or recognition of his achievements. He has never worked hard to gain attention. I never thought that it was part of his genes.'

'Well,' said Shubhojit, 'this is the happiest day of my life, Ma! My children have made an attempt to understand my passion for work. Hopefully, they will not misunderstand me any longer, or at least make some allowances for me.'

'Misunderstand? Oh no, never again!' said Hemant with tears in his eyes. 'Papa, I was only angry with you for not giving our mother even a small portion of your time. We could have been much better off in our personal lives.'

'Yes,' said Shubhojit. 'I shall never forgive myself for that. I wish I could still make amends, I hope an opportunity comes my way.'

'Maybe, you still can, Papa!' said Neelakshi. 'Who knows?'

22

Given the circumstances in which she had found herself, Yashodhra had acted for what she thought was her best option when she decided to leave Shubhojit but, at times now, she found herself in an exasperating situation. There was a constant struggle between her mind and heart. She had been restraining herself from visiting Shubhojit and her children for fear of upsetting Manidhar. But, she was constantly worrying about Shubhojit's health and her children's future. Manidhar was quick to notice this. Yashodhra's absent-mindedness made him lose his temper and inevitably led to unpleasant arguments between them. Shubhojit's illness and Yashodhra's preoccupation with her former family had shattered the peace in their home. Manidhar found it hard to accept this new reality, and he could no longer take it. He opposed any suggestion by Yashodhra about visiting Shubhojit's house.

'Haven't you had enough of them, Yashodhra? Leave them alone. They are perfectly capable of taking care of themselves. Leave your past behind and move ahead with me.'

'Why don't you try to understand, Manidhar?' Yashodhra would retort in temper. 'It is basic human courtesy. The heavens are not going to fall if I visit them occasionally to reassure myself of their well-being. In fact, it would be a gracious gesture if you were to come along at least once.'

'Oh, forget it, Yashodhra! These are your liabilities and your emotional compulsions. Don't drag me into them. Isn't it enough that I haven't stopped you from going there? I could have put my foot down, you know.'

'Oh, could you really? I am not your bonded labourer. I am an individual, with my own rights. I shall take my own decisions. You have no right to stop me. Don't you dare even try it, Manidhar!' Yashodhra was seething.

'Then, why talk about it? Do whatever you feel like. Don't pester me about these things. I don't believe in living in the past. I like to look towards the future and move ahead.'

'Well, the difference between the present and the past is only of a moment, and so is the difference between the present and the future. In either case, one can't break ties in a matter of minutes!'

'Well, you did!'

'Oh, shut up and go to hell!'

'Mind your words!'

'Mind your attitude! You will be a lonely man one day, with no past, present or future.'

'I wouldn't be roaming around with a begging bowl, certainly.'

Manidhar slammed the door and went out leaving Yashodhra in tears. It was hard for her to accept his attitude. 'Has he outgrown his feelings for me? Or is his behaviour just a manifestation of his insecurity? Is he still jealous or is it pure indifference, and he doesn't care either way?'

Yashodhra sat in a despondent mood. Whatever Manidhar's reasons, she had made up her mind to go and visit Shubhojit, Hemant and Neelakshi. She told the driver to drop her at Shubhojit's house and pick her up in the evening. She walked along the driveway, crossed the veranda admiring the beautiful flowers, entered through the front door, climbed the stairs and made her appearance on the balcony. Breakfast was over and the family was settling down for another round of information-sharing.

'Hi, Mom! Great to see you!' Hemant and Neelakshi rushed forward to welcome their mother.

'What a pleasant surprise!' Shubhojit expressed his happiness. Yashodhra greeted Shubhojit's mother, who nodded with a smile.

'How are you doing, Shubhojit? Taking rest seems to be doing good for you.'

'Yes! I feel relaxed and much better.'

'Mom, Dadima has been telling us about our village and the life that she spent there as a young woman,' said Neelakshi. 'It is such an eye-opener. She is a storehouse of tales and experiences!'

'What a contrast between village life and city life, in almost every sphere!' said Hemant. 'It is wonderful to know about these things and it also gives an insight into how society has developed to where it is today.'

'I think I have come at the right time!' said Yashodhra.

'I have already told you about the morning schedule of a village woman,' said Kamladevi. 'Now, let me take it forward from there. There were two things that were always done in the *haara*...'

'And what was that, Dadima?'

'It was a large, deep bowl made of mud into which upalas, broken into fours, were stacked in three or four layers and lit. The fire would catch slowly. On it was placed a *kadawni*, a big earthen pot with a thick bottom, for heating some of the morning milk. A sieve-like cover was put over it to prevent it from boiling over. The milk was kept simmering until evening, when it would turn light pink in colour and have a thick layer of malai. The malai was a treat for the children and they loved it. The rest of the milk was used for drinking or for making curds,' said Kamladevi.

'I can almost imagine it, Dadima!' said Hemant, 'Papa! Do you remember the taste of that malai?'

'How can I forget it?' smiled Shubhojit. 'We used to mix the malai with sarson ka saag during the winter or mix it with gur, that is, jaggery or shakkar, and eat it with a roti. It tasted great and was truly unforgettable. No pizzas or burgers of yours can match its taste or nutritional value.'

'The evening meal,' said Kamladevi, 'used to be prepared the same way. We used to call it *randheen* and it was the main meal of the day. Randheen meant that it was allowed to simmer on a low fire for a long time. In summer, it used to be wheat-porridge; in winter, bajre ki khichdi; the rest of the year, dal-chawal khichdi. The slow, simmering process made it delicious. It was also easy and convenient for womenfolk to prepare after a day's hard work. That was our regular food and the meal used to be over before it was dark.'

'How interesting!' said Neelakshi. 'It is so similar to the Western concept of supper! They have their evening meal by seven o'clock.'

'That's what our health freaks advise these days,' said Hemant. 'They say that carbohydrates should be eaten at least two to three hours before going to sleep, to allow the food to get digested. It also helps keep weight under control.'

'Rotis made of wheat, gram or bajra, and vegetables were made only for guests,' continued. Kamladevi. 'Wheat flour was used for special guests and the chapatis made of it were called *maande*. But they were not a regular feature in most households. Most of our utensils were made of a metal alloy, with copper, bronze and brass being the main elements. They were considered as being more hygienic than other utensils which came much later.'

'I remember, Ma,' said Shubhojit, 'only we had a teapot, cups and saucers. And these were often borrowed and used by our neighbours, whenever they had guests.'

'Yes, Shubhojit,' said Kamladevi, 'those were great times! We lived together; helped one another, believed in community effort and existed in harmony with each other and with nature. Jealousy did not have much of a place in relationships. Of course, families did have their own share of fights, but that was a different matter altogether.'

'Our summer vacations used to be such fun, Ma!' said Shubhojit. 'We would finish our morning meal by nine o'clock, and then the elders would ask us to take our cattle, generally buffaloes or cows, to the fields for grazing. The dung provided a protective covering for the bare feet against hot sand at the time of return around afternoons.'

'Yuck! Didn't you feel dirty smearing your feet with dung?' asked Neelakshi.

'Oh! It was a part of life. Your papa was very good at collecting the dung before it fell on the ground,' chuckled Kamladevi with a mischievous look in her eyes.

'And you didn't even wash it clean?' asked a curious Hemant.

'Oh! We did,' said Shubojit. 'We took the buffalo to the village pond, gave it a bath, took a shot at swimming too; that was a part of our daily routine. The pond used to be full of cattle and boys; and there seemed no difference between them. We did not bother about things like hygiene, cleanliness or impurities in water. We never ever suffered from the after-effects of such things, either.'

'On the contrary,' laughed Kamladevi, 'any child who fell ill got a thrashing from the elders in the family. Falling sick was a sign of a weak constitution.'

'Oh, God, Papa! You and your culture!' smiled Neelakshi.

'Hemant, you have heard of shepherds,' said Shubhojit. 'They were called *paali* in our lingo. One such man called Deepu—I still remember his name—used to look after the cattle of our village. There was a small forest—we used to call it *bani*—a little away from the pond. The shepherd would take the herd, for which the local name was *lehnda*, numbering about two to three hundred, to the bani, where they grazed and rested till the evening. He would take his food along and keep an eye on the animals the whole day. By and by, the cattle too got trained,' laughed Shubhojit.

Hemant, disbelieving, asked, 'Trained to do what?'

'The shepherd would gather the cattle at dusk and lead them back to the village. You will be surprised to know that they knew exactly which road to take and, as soon as they entered the village, at which house to stop. They would come back as a herd, and each would take just the right turn to its own house. It was amazing and so uncanny!'

'Papa, did you too go to the bani any time?' asked Hemant, who sensed the thrill of adventure in this activity.

'Of course, we did! Almost daily! During vacations, we used to spend the whole day in the bani with our friends. After school hours, evening time would be playtime and the bani offered a variety of games. There were many jaal trees, which bore a lot of fruit called *peel-pichu* during the summer. I don't know what they are called here, but we used to eat a lot of them. They were very colourful, almost crimson in colour. The jaal trees were very friendly, as I recall.'

Neelakshi asked, 'In what way were they friendly?'

'Their branches hung low and were flexible, and they never broke. There were no thorns or sharp curves. As far as I can remember, we used to climb up the trees, swing on the branches, and jump down without any risk of hurting ourselves. That's why we called them "friendly" trees,' said Shubhojit.

'Oh, Papa! I think I know what you are talking about,' said Neelakshi excitedly. 'Perhaps, this is the sort of tree that Robert Frost talks about in the poem called *Birches*. In it, he also refers to a shepherd boy who goes to the forest every day and swings on its branches. Robert Frost draws a subtle comparison between the rural and the urban divide, too, in this poem. He is so enamoured of this tree that he wants to go to heaven while swinging on its branches, stay there for a little while and come back to the earth, descending on its branches because he says... I forget the lines.'

'Because,' quoted Yashodhra, '"Earth's the right place for love." Do I remember correctly, Neelakshi?' smiled Yashodhra.

'Oh, Mom! I forgot literature was your subject. Of course you would remember! And Robert Frost is one of your favourite poets.'

'That takes me back to my forest memories,' said Shubhojit. 'Those were the days. We didn't have the slightest care or worry in the world. Our time in the bani was spent in total bliss. We were in complete harmony with nature then without even realizing it. I dream of going back to that kind of a life where one lives simply, in natural surroundings, and with basic needs satisfied.'

'Are you people offering me lunch or not?' asked Yashodhra

with a smile. 'I am so hungry even though I have only been listening. What about Shubhojit and his mother who have been talking for so long? They must be starving. Let's call Bahadur.'

Lunch was a satisfying spread, as always. Bahadur took special care when Yashodhra memsahib was around. It was chhole-puri, bhalle and palak-paneer for Hemant, Neelakshi and Yashodhra; steamed vegetables and yellow-dal-tadka for Shubhojit. Kamladevi could have her pick of whatever she wanted. There was salad and buttermilk for all.

The lunch hour continued longer than usual. No one was in a hurry as they were enjoying the food and the companionship, morsel by morsel, and moment by moment. The time, the circumstances and the present company—all were conducive to a feeling of contentment and peace.

Lunch over, Yashodhra contemplated making a move and going for some window-shopping. She felt she had overstayed her visit. Sensing her embarrassment, Hemant came up with a suggestion: 'Mom, let's go and have a cup of coffee at a cafe and then I will drop you back.'

'Coffee, yes, certainly! I would love it but I'll call my driver after that and go for some shopping. You guys can come back or catch up with your friends,' said Yashodhra.

As she picked up her bag and took leave of them, Shubhojit smiled at her and said, 'Thank you, Yashodhra! Come again if you can!'

She nodded as Hemant and Neelakshi accompanied her towards the door.

23

SHUBHOJIT STOOD in the balcony, watching Yashodhra being escorted by Hemant and Neelakshi towards their car; watching her quick, graceful steps, the warm radiance of her fair face and the charm of her personality. There had always been a sense of purpose about her even while she had been with him. Her assured look had exercised a spell over him in earlier days.

She was exactly his idea of what a lady should be: simple, elegant, beautiful and intelligent. There was a sort of magic about her, a kind of glow in the air around her. He was appalled that he had failed to notice all this when they were together. He had taken her for granted! He had not had the time or even the inclination to be with her. And the result was that he had lost her, and that too to an undeserving fellow. Whether in a fit of anger or frustration or on the rebound, she had chosen to exchange the security and status of her position for the false glamour and glitz as personified by Manidhar.

Shubhojit felt that Yashodhra too realized now that she had made a mistake but it was too late, and the awkward situation made them avoid all reference to it. She had been full of a youthful zest for life, which he had misinterpreted as a thirst for luxury and novelty. With her buoyant and vivacious spirit, she had only wanted to breathe some fresh air into the ossified and stereotyped routine of their stifling official life.

'What right had I to force her to believe what I myself believed in? Had I really been interested in fostering individual growth and its role in human relationships? Had I given her enough space? Hadn't I bogged her down in my own ideologies and culture till she crumbled under their weight?' Shubhojit continued in his contemplative mood. 'And now, a gulf lies between us: a gulf in the shape of Manidhar, social moorings and a sense of delicate balance. It won't be easy to cross it or bury it and start anew.'

The enforced, passive life was beginning to bore him at times. He had been a man of action even in the midst of insipid files and the administrative maze. It was a tough time for him, physically and emotionally. The compulsive bed rest seemed to have done him good as far as his body was concerned, but his mind and heart were pulling him in opposite directions. He considered himself lucky that he had his mother and children staying with him. Even Yashodhra's behaviour towards him, at the risk of damaging her domestic happiness, had been unexpected.

Shubhojit was lost in the quiet world of his thoughts, when Bahadur came to inform him of Adishankar's arrival.

'Send him up to my room. And make tea and some snacks!' Shubhojit tidied himself and pulled a chair near his bed.

'How are you, Sir? It has been a long time! Great to see you looking so good!' Adishankar shook hands with Shubhojit.

'What's new in office, Adi?' asked Shubhojit.

Adishankar smiled. 'Well, Sir! We are always neck-deep in work. Our office work is like a habit; we can neither change it nor get rid of it. There is no option but to continue as long as we can. Do you miss office, Sir?'

'In a way, yes!' said Shubhojit. 'It gives a sense of purpose in life. Imagine getting up in the morning and having nothing to look forward to! It can be depressing!'

'Sir, you have achieved so much in your professional life. Aren't you happy? Aren't you tired? I am sure every man reaches a saturation point.'

'I am pleased with my professional achievements. The struggle to attain them has been worth it, especially the relentless, uphill task of reaching the top. But I feel that I am not done yet. I haven't come to the end of the road, I have to carry on a little longer. I haven't finished working for the welfare of humanity. I wouldn't be happy otherwise.'

'Sir, what struggle are you talking about? We are past the stage of struggle. We are at a decision-making level where we can help formulate policies and give a new direction to the existing thought processes.'

'True! Maybe the struggle is within me and I want to fight till all my passion for work has been fully satisfied. I still want to work for and with my fellow men, and help them find a solution for their problems.'

'Sir, I can only hope to emulate your ideals and determination to march ahead undeterred!' Adishankar's eyes were full of admiration.

'I want to reach that ultimate level of commitment and dedication where I can entertain a well-deserved satisfaction of doing enough and contributing my bit. Then, I can consider retiring from this world of men and mundane affairs and renouncing the luxuries and comforts of this life. I would like to be one with the elements of nature; where I breathe the essence of the godhead in every living thing, animate or inanimate…'

'Sir, your illness has turned you into a philosopher!' Adishankar tried to lighten the conversation.

Shubhojit laughed with a sense of resignation. 'Don't worry,

Adi! I haven't reached that level of cynicism as yet. Hemant and Neelakshi are far from settled. One can't run away from family responsibilities.'

'Sir, I have really enjoyed talking to you today! Can I take your leave now?'

'Yes, of course! Come again, Adi!'

'I shall, Sir. And thank you for the tea and snacks!'

The next morning started in much the same way. Kamladevi, lively as ever, asked the children: 'Are you bored with my village stories or still interested in them?'

'Bored?' asked Hemant. 'Not at all, Dadima! Where else would we get such a personal account of rural society and of the life of the villagers?'

'We have only text-book knowledge of it. Hearing about it from somebody who has actually lived through it is so different,' said Neelakshi, 'and that too our own grandmother!'

'Not only your grandmother, Neelu!' said Shubhojit. 'I too lived that life when I was a child. My entire childhood was spent in that set-up. I still remember that there were at least four elderly men in our extended family who were like our grandfather. They wielded the same authority and had equal rights over all the children. There was no concept of who was whose grandchild. They were the patronizing elders who could scold anyone or tell them to do any work. For instance, if I was going to the village well for bathing and washing my clothes, they could ask me to take their laundry too and wash it. Nobody would mind as there was an atmosphere of total cooperation.'

'Papa, you used to bathe in the village pond or at the well? There were no bathrooms in the houses?' asked Neelakshi.

'No, though there was a bathroom in our haveli, it was not

usual,' said Kamladevi. 'The women would bathe in a metal tub in some corner of the house, placing three or four cots around to serve as a curtain. However, everyone had to go out into the fields to relieve themselves—a totally open defecation system. Women went out in groups in the early morning before light or late in the evenings after it became dark. It was the accepted thing those days. Everybody would be aware and careful. Men, of course, would go out for everything: they roamed about in the mornings, brushing their teeth with a neem-stick; went to the well for a bath. For men, and women too, it was community living to the nth degree. They were unfamiliar with the concept of a personal life. Children of both sexes bathed in the small canal running by the side of the village. People remained content in their own world and hardly made an effort to intrude into forbidden areas. There were fewer husband-and-wife problems and the bond between them lasted well into old age.'

'Of course, there were always a few cases of somebody's wife having an affair—or what you call these days, being in a relationship—with someone else's husband,' interrupted Shubhojit. 'Such stories were not unheard of. They were a part of the ground reality and, at times, were accepted as normal.'

'Really, Papa?' asked Hemant.

'Well, certain things were accepted as part of the culture,' said Kamladevi. 'For instance, the physical intimacy between the *devar*, that is, the husband's younger brother and the bhabhi, the sister-in-law. People accepted it as a normal practice. It was not considered scandalous nor did it raise an eyebrow. That kind of escapade was not unknown. But, one would never hear of these things in the case of the *jaith*, that is, the husband's elder brother and the younger brother's wife. It is also true that there were instances of intimacy between the father-in-law and the daughter-in-law. These were more common in families where the main earning member was in the army and away from home for long spells. The mother-in-law often fought with her husband for his excessive fondness for or indulgence towards the daughter-in-law.'

'Horrible, isn't it, Papa?' responded Hemant, whereas Neelakshi made an attempt to hide her sense of discomfiture.

'Hemant, most of the time, it was based on convenience,' said Shubhojit, who liked to have a man-to-man conversation with his son. 'The men did not suffer from a sense of shame in these matters. For them, these were escapades which held an element of adventure. The tough working conditions, the few opportunities they had of intimacy with their wives, and the nigh-impossibility of having a natural, healthy relationship with women—all this led to a repression of emotions which then found a natural outlet with whoever was available.'

'Papa! Are you justifying such conduct or practices? If it happens in cities, everyone condemns it as a vice prevalent in towns and cities. If it takes place in villages, it is accepted as normal and natural?' said Hemant.

'How hypocritical!' exclaimed Neelakshi.

Kamladevi had been listening silently. Since this was being discussed openly, she decided to let out another truth.

'I shall tell you something more interesting,' she said, looking at the children. 'Many times, these escapades took place in the fields. There used to be many women from the lower castes working as labourers in the fields. Some of them were quite good-looking. The landowner kept a close eye on them and whenever he got a chance, he would pick up one and have a good time with her. People laughed whenever they saw a handsome boy among the lower-caste people. They guessed that he must be the offspring of someone from a higher caste. These affairs were always discussed in whispers and then dismissed with a wave of the hand.'

Shubhojit said, 'Ma, I remember Hazari, the elderly man in our thola, who was notorious. They said he would try his luck with every woman and then boast about his adventures.'

Kamladevi laughed aloud without any embarrassment. She was happy that such things were being discussed openly in front of the children. All this was a part of the reality of village life and was best discussed as being normal. Hemant and Neelakshi were no longer children. They needed to know and discuss everything with their parents. It was a part of the growing-up process. For Shubhojit too, it had been a rare opportunity to talk about all this with his children. It was necessary for parents to talk to their children as adults.

Hemant and Neelakshi were getting restless. They had learnt enough for the day. It was almost lunch time and they looked for some respite from the hard facts of life.

'What a life, Hemant!' said Neelakshi.

'What do you mean?'

'A life full of hardships, trials, tribulations but not without a hint of romance or adventure.'

'In their own way, yes!'

'Human instinct and nature remain the same, isn't that so? Only time, age and opportunities differ. I listened to nothing that really startled me.'

'Really?'

'Have we changed in any way, I mean, in the present day?'

'Yes, in science, technology and the usage of modern gadgets!'

'But, human nature remains essentially the same!'
'Yes, the same!'
They nodded in agreement.

24

*T*HERE WAS a slight drizzle that day. Maybe it was a precursor of the monsoon season. It had been extremely hot for a few days and it was hoped that the rain would bring a respite from the scorching heat.

'Everyone looks forward to the monsoon in India,' thought Shubhojit. 'That is the season when the cruelty of the sun is mellowed by the magnanimity of the rain god. The parched earth gets a thorough drenching with the rainwater and emanates a refreshing smell that soothes the senses. The wilting leaves get a new lease of life and turn green once again. The sparrows and other birds no longer go thirsty, they hop around bathing in pools of water. Everything around looks young, happy and fresh! It is the beginning of a new cycle in nature, so very endearing to humans. And, above all, it is the boon that the farmers have been looking forward to so eagerly, lest their newly planted fields get parched up.'

'Isn't it true in our case too,' Shubhojit continued thinking, 'even society? Times change, as do the generations, as well as our customs, but certain things remain essentially the same.'

The talks with his mother had taken him back into the past. He had lost track of time and the awareness of its transient nature: he didn't realize he had come so far, almost to the fag end of his active life journey. There had been no time for him even to think of initiating a link between the new generation and its roots.

'But then, who is responsible for it? The present generation only looks ahead without realizing that its ties with the past are slowly breaking up.'

For the first time in his life, Shubhojit felt concerned. He was pleased that Hemant and Neelakshi had taken an interest in their grandmother's heartfelt description of village life, and her account of how their family had come up and made a mark in life. 'At least, they are now better aware of their antecedents,' thought Shubhojit.

Hemant had only a few days left before he had to report back to his law school, but, Neelakshi could take it easy with her college for a couple of weeks more. Kamladevi had never felt so wanted by her own family members. She had told them whatever she knew and whatever they wanted to know.

This day, too, had started the same way as the others. In fact, the rain had brought in some freshness and it was a little more pleasant. The congregation of family members began in the morning after their heartily enjoyed breakfast.

'There was a lot of community development and participation by the people in the village,' Kamladevi continued without a preamble. 'We worked in unison and collectively undertook physical works. I have already told you about the working of the kolhu and the winnowing of wheat which was done with everyone's active cooperation. Almost all the critical decisions were taken by the panchayat, which constituted a body of the most respected persons in the village. Its moral authority to adjudicate social issues was unquestioned, and its decisions were the final word.'

'Yes! We know about it,' said Hemant. 'We have read Munshi Premchand's story, *Panch Parmeshwar*. And we know about "Juman Sheikh" and his moment of enlightenment when it is his turn to be in a position of power. It is the sense of justice and fair play that must reign supreme over all personal interests.'

Kamladevi seemed impressed: 'I am happy you understood the moral of that story,' she said. 'Our panchayat had its own system, its own set of rules and methods of arriving at decisions. I remember how it dealt with the problem of siltation in a village pond. Unlike the present day, dependence on the government was minimal. Once, during the summer season, when the water had dried up in one of the ponds, it was noticed that there had been quite a substantial silt deposit, thereby reducing its water storage capacity. A pond full of water was a lifeline for the villagers and the cattle, and this problem needed immediate attention. They couldn't be assured of an immediate response from the government.'

'I remember that situation very well, Ma!' Shubhojit interrupted. 'I, too, did my bit in digging and making it deeper.'

'Yes, my dear!' smiled Kamladevi. 'It was concluded that the pond had to be dug deeper to increase its storage capacity. A plan was drawn up for doing it quickly and smoothly. Every family had to do voluntary labour: each *taagdi* would excavate and remove two *baadhas* of silt. This was a panchayat *farman* conveyed by the beating of the drum by the village chowkidar.'

'What is a taagdi, Dadima?' asked Neelakshi.

'A taagdi is a black thread worn around the waist by men. If a family had four male members, it meant that it had four taagdis,' explained Kamladevi.

'And, what is a baadha?' asked Hemant.

'That is a unit of measurement. One baadha meant an area that was 10 feet long, 10 feet wide and 1 foot deep, that is, about 100 cubic feet of silt or soil, whatever you may call it,' said Kamladevi.

'Simply put, each male member from every family of the village was expected to excavate and remove 200 cubic feet of silt from the pond-bed. And if any one member was physically unable to do so, his family members would do his part or get it done from any other person. The rule of exemptions did not operate here,' explained Shubhojit.

'That is how the village community used to assert itself,' said Kamladevi, 'using common labour and contribution towards solving problems. The results were almost instant and long-lasting.'

'The self-sufficiency of the system,' said Hemant, 'is really an example worth emulating, Dadima. I can understand how the structure of society evolved through the ages into a political set-up. Even for the most advanced world democracies, it was the village society that laid the foundation for their political systems and ideologies.'

'I would like to tell you a little about a family's social standing,' said Kamladevi. 'It was generally assessed from the number of persons it could host at a given time. And that depended on the number of cots and the bed linen that a family possessed. The baithak had to contain at least fifteen or twenty cots along with the bed linen. It was a symbol of social status, and signified a family's *uth-baith*, meaning social relations, in society.'

'It sounds so strange, Dadima!' said Neelakshi. 'Cots in the drawing room! And as a symbol of social status? It is so different from today's life where we go to any lengths to decorate our drawing room with artefacts collected from different corners of the country.'

'But your drawing rooms are hardly used, as they are just ornamental now,' said Kamladevi. 'It is probably the decor that makes it a symbol of your social status.'

'People were not hard pressed for time. When a person visited his close friends in an adjoining village, he would stay overnight. People normally walked anywhere between two to five miles for honouring social bonds,' said Shubhojit. 'And anybody who walked that distance to meet with friends would naturally stay and eat with them. This was called roti ka sambandh. It was considered an insult if that person had his meals anywhere else or with any other family in the village.'

'These customs appear funny and weird at first,' said Hemant, 'but when you think about the logic behind them, they come out as both natural and pragmatic. In fact, they are statements of practical wisdom of our ancestors. I wonder if theirs was a generation in search of the future, or is that true only of us.'

'I feel it is our generation that is in search of the future which, perhaps, lies in the lessons learnt from our past,' said Neelakshi.

Shubhojit smiled at the depth of Hemant's thoughts and the appropriateness of his observation. He noticed a marked change in his son's attitude and behaviour since he had fallen sick. Hemant had matured beyond his years in a short span of time.

'You will be surprised to know, Neelu,' said Kamladevi, 'that the concept of gender discrimination can be traced to our times even in the case of cattle.'

'Oh, my God! Gender discrimination in animals?' laughed Neelakshi.

'Yes, my dear!' smiled Kamladevi. 'You know by now that cattle occupied a place of importance in family life since tractors had not come into use by then. The ox was the most important because most of the agricultural operations were dependent on him: ploughing the land as well as for transporting men or material. He was even fed desi ghee in winter.'

'Oh, goodness! Ox and desi ghee?' laughed Hemant and Neelakshi. 'Which animal was more popular, Dadima, the cow or the buffalo?'

'Well, between the two, the buffalo was a higher milk-yielding animal and was much more in demand. Today's cross-bred cows were not heard of during our times,' said Kamladevi.

Hemant and Neelakshi were amazed at their grandmother's general knowledge while Shubhojit simply smiled. He knew his mother and her sound rustic common sense.

'But Dadima, you spoke of gender discrimination in animals. What was that?' asked Neelakshi.

'I am coming to that,' replied Kamladevi. 'In the case of a buffalo, the female calf, which would grow into a milk-yielding animal, and therefore, was more useful in domestic life, was always more welcome than a male calf. The usefulness of a male calf was limited. If a male buffalo calf died, nobody cared much about it, but the loss of a female calf was nothing short of a tragedy. As regards to a cow, the male calf was much more welcome and looked after because it would grow into a hardworking ox. Now, don't you think that that counts as gender bias?'

'Certainly, it does, Dadima!' said Neelakshi. 'Only because the female buffalo calf and the male cow calf were more useful, they were welcome and cared for. Wasn't that a totally utilitarian approach towards life?'

'It was! No doubt about that!' said Kamladevi in a sombre tone. 'This was true even in our case. A woman, too, was treated well only when she was pregnant. She was given good food to eat and pampered in every way possible. This continued as long as she was feeding her baby, after which things would go back to the old routine. This was the accepted practice during our times and we endured it all without any complaint. We considered it to be our destiny. We were brought up to think and believe the same way.'

'But things have certainly changed, Dadima,' said Hemant, 'and for the better as far as women are concerned. Isn't it?'

'Oh, yes, definitely as far as girls are concerned,' Kamladevi was emphatic, 'but things have deteriorated in general in the villages.'

'What do you mean?'

'The community bonhomie and cooperation is a thing of the past nowadays,' said Shubhojit. 'The village culture, too, witnessed a drastic change in the late '60s and '70s. Earlier, whenever I visited the village during my summer vacations, I would be offered a glass of milk in every house that I visited. I remember a particular occasion when I had to drink fourteen glasses of milk in a matter of an hour and a half. The women in the different households were like a grandmother or an aunt or an elderly relative, and I could not refuse. But, on my next visit after about five years, I was politely and affectionately asked if I would like to have a cup of tea. I was quite taken aback by the element of formality that had crept into village culture. I noticed another change. Consumption of liquor had been almost a social taboo and was frowned upon till the late '60s, thanks to the Arya Samaj movement in our area. Fear of authority or what may be better expressed as Sarkar ka Iqbal, ruled, perhaps because the memories of British Raj had not faded entirely. One constable could come and round up the whole village. But now, the situation is such that one should not be surprised or shocked if a whole police contingent got beaten up by the villagers, and the police weren't able to assert any semblance of authority!' Shubhojit was very articulate in expressing his dismay.

'Oh, Papa, isn't change a natural phenomenon in life?' said Neelakshi. 'Certain things change for the good, others for worse, perhaps! Both, though, are relative terms. If things didn't change, there would be no progress. The same principle applies even to rural culture.'

'Let's not discuss what and where things have gone wrong in the villages too,' said Hemant, 'or even probe into the reasons for it. Dadima has told us things about which we knew nothing. It has been amazing to get to know about one's past: an era which was rich in heritage, value system, culture and traditions. We can be proud of its antiquity and its solid foundation on which rests our modern magnificent edifice. Now, we know our roots better. Nobody can take away from us the glory of our past. We can look back to it for inspiration and guidance, and we can connect with our roots.'

'Our soil is sacred, Papa!' said Neelakshi, clearly overwhelmed by Hemant's emotional outburst, 'and its scent is so strong and pleasant that we want to keep on inhaling it till our lungs are full of it; abundant and clear.'

Shubhojit smiled and looked at Kamladevi whose eyes were brimming with tears. He knew that those tears stemmed from nostalgia and pure joy.

25

It was cloudy the whole day. The wind had been blowing hard since morning and it had driven away the rain clouds by the afternoon, after which the sky was overcast once again. The rain came down sharp in the late afternoon and the trees were wet and dripping. The dry autumn foliage threw off the summer heat and swung gently with the raindrops. The sun peeped out from behind the clouds every now and then and left in its wake a rainbow that made the sky look radiant.

Hemant and Neelakshi went to the window and looked out. It was still drizzling. Tiny pools had formed in the rear lawn, in which sparrows splashed with joy. The leaves on the large jamun tree glistened when the intermittent sunlight fell on them.

'How beautiful it is outside!' said Neelakshi.

'Everything looks so clean and pure, having been bathed in rainwater,' said Kamladevi. 'As young girls, we would love to go out in the rain, get wet, dance and run around our big haveli and have fun with the others. We would make *gulgulas* and malpuas and eat to our hearts' content.'

'Dadima!' smiled Hemant. 'You were and still are quite a romantic at heart.'

Shubhojit had been listening quietly. The conversation during the past one week about village life had gradually restored his mental equilibrium and softened his heart once again. He felt as if the rain outside had had a chastening effect even on his mental state. He no longer had those feelings of resentment, bitterness and frustration that had been harbouring in him for some time. But, now, the rain was slowing down and it seemed as if the sky might clear in an hour or so. It was just the right weather for hot, lip-smacking snacks and cups of coffee before carrying on with their conversation.

The rain-washed surroundings looked beautiful in the evening. The mellowing light of the setting sun lent radiance to the clear blue sky. Kamladevi, Shubhojit, Hemant and Neelakshi sat together, enjoying the ambience and relishing the snacks. Shubhojit was in a particularly good mood. Remembering a story, he smiled.

'Papa, you are thinking of something,' said Hemant, 'and I am sure it is either funny or pleasant. You are smiling at the very thought of it!'

'Yes,' said Shubhojit, 'and I must share it with you all. It will amuse you. It is the rain that has reminded me of an incident about which I heard from others.'

'Go on, don't make us wait now, Papa!' said Neelakshi.

'Shubhojit, I too want to know!' said Kamladevi.

'It is about a certain Kanhaiyalal. He had joined service as a *naib tahsildar* on the eve of Independence and, after a long career, retired as *tahsildar*. He had served more than the stipulated number of years because there was no record of his date of birth. He used to boast that he would retire in his own sweet time because nobody could check out his date of birth.'

'Papa, he sounds interesting!'

'Oh, very much so!' replied Shubhojit. 'He was an extremely handsome man and dressed smartly in a stark white shirt, trousers, a black tie and a turban.'

'He must have cut a fine figure, Papa!' said Neelakshi.

'And a stylish one!' said Hemant.

'He was aware of his own good appearance,' said Shubhojit, 'and took a lot of pride in it.'

'Go on, Papa!'

Shubhojit said, 'You might have heard of the river Ghaggar. It is a seasonal river and flows along the border between Punjab and Haryana. It is known for its annual floods during the monsoon. My story dates back to when Punjab was still an undivided state. Floods caused by the Ghaggar had led to a complete destruction of standing crops and marooned a number of villages falling under Kanhaiyalal's jurisdiction.'

'What does that mean, Papa?'

'That meant that some of the villages turned into islands and were completely surrounded by water. The biggest loss was that of the harvest which was totally ruined. The government announced a number of relief measures as well as a supply of food and rations to the villages, besides financial compensation to the villagers.'

'What had Kanhaiyalal to do with all this?'

'Kanhaiyalal was an important person. He was the tahsildar and, hence, responsible for the distribution of all relief to the affected people. He withdrew the total financial compensation in the form of cash, decided to go to the village and distribute it among the villagers.'

'Well, it seems fair and square till now, Papa!'

'Yes, it does, my dear! He came home and exchanged the cash.'

'Exchanged? For what?'

'He kept the genuine currency notes at home and filled his briefcase with nakli (counterfeit) ones.'

'Oh, my God!' exclaimed Neelakshi while Kamladevi merely smiled.

'Then, he had to wade through neck-deep water to reach the people across the other end, keeping the briefcase on his head. He took great strides in the water and was almost halfway through when, suddenly, he slipped and, along with the briefcase, went under the water. The briefcase was knocked open. The currency notes spilled out and started floating on the surface of the water while the villagers stood mute witness to the incident.'

'Perhaps, that's what Kanhaiyalal wanted,' said Kamladevi.

'Exactly!' said Shubhojit. 'That was his plan. The villagers waiting at the other end were all shocked and sympathised with the 'poor' tahsildar. He reached across somehow and spun out a drama. With tears in his eyes, he cried in a trembling voice, "How can I show my face to you all? This Ghaggar has eaten up the relief and compensation amount. I can atone my sins only by committing suicide as I alone am accountable. How shall I compensate for this loss? I must jump into the river and end my life." Kanhaiyalal went on and on, till all his tears dried up. He looked at the baffled faces of the innocent villagers, mischievously and calculatingly.'

'What happened next, Papa?' asked Neelakshi.

'Well, Kanhaiyalal, shrewd as he was,' said Shubhojit, 'had his finger on the pulse of the people. All through his carefully manipulated drama, he had been closely observing their faces. He knew his emotional outburst was going straight to their hearts and arousing their sympathy. He knew he could fully exploit their feelings.'

'How interesting!' Hemant asked curiously, 'So, what was the outcome?'

'The people were taken in by his stratagem. They caught hold of him and made him sit down. Then they came up with a proposal. They assured him that he did not need to worry about the money. They would give statements, with their thumb impressions, that each of them had received his share of the compensation. The government did not have to get an inkling of the real situation and Kanhaiyalal would not have to face any charges for negligence.'

'What a master brain!' said Hemant.

'No doubt about that!' said Shubhojit. 'As soon as he heard this proposal, he burst out, "I don't know how I shall ever repay your generosity! I shall remain indebted to you my whole life." Kanhaiyalal continued to work on the simple and innocent minds of the villagers till he was absolutely satisfied that his sweet words had had the desired impact. In a matter of an hour or two, the villagers did as they had proposed: A list of all the people was drawn up, in which they put their signatures or their thumb impressions, stating that they had received compensation from the government for the loss of their crops as a result of the floods.'

'What a crook!' said Neelakshi.

'Well, he got the money as well as the goodwill of the people,' said Shubhojit. 'He also managed to hoodwink the government. I shall give you another example of his resourcefulness.'

'I see that the Kanhaiyalal saga is not yet complete,' smiled Neelakshi.

'Gradually,' said Shubhojit, 'Kanhaiyalal came to acquire a lot of clout in political circles. He became close to the then-chief minister of the state, who invited Prime Minister Indira Gandhi to visit one of the districts. Kanhaiyalal happened to be posted there as tahsildar and was entrusted with certain responsibilities regarding her visit. He had a large welcome gate installed across the highway, at the entrance to the town and got little girls to sit on top of the structure in such a way that they were hidden from public view. As Indira Gandhi's open jeep passed underneath the welcome gate, they showered her with flowers. The Prime Minister was deeply touched by this gesture.'

'Ingenious, certainly!' said Neelakshi.

'Well, he didn't stop at that,' said Shubhojit. 'Indira Gandhi was scheduled to visit the next district and Kanhaiyalal decided to present to her some of the local, aromatic basmati rice. He had twenty bags of rice spread out on a sheet and deputed fifty women to handpick the unbroken rice and got two or three bags of it. The chief minister was asked to present one of these bags to Mrs Gandhi.'

'What purpose did it serve, Papa?' asked Hemant.

'In about less than a month,' smiled Shubhojit, 'there came a request for more rice from the PMO—that is, the Prime Minister's Office—and Kanhaiyalal found himself in demand. He arranged to send the second bag. He did not want to send a few bags in one go: the demand had to remain fresh, and so too, his importance. He boasted about having a direct connection to the highest office of the country. Kanhaiyalal had established himself as a very important person.'

'Well, his tactics brought him rich dividends Papa,' said Neelakshi. 'He was clearly a man who knew the ways of the world and made the best of the situations that came his way.'

'My seniors told me that he considered his collector's orders sacrosanct and ensured strict compliance with them,' continued Shubhojit. 'It is said that one of his collectors commented in his Annual Confidential Report that "he was the most useful scoundrel he had ever come across in his life". He had an uncanny ability to turn adversities into advantages, along with a talent for winning people over by his sweet, polite words that melted their hearts.'

Shubhojit continued, 'When we joined the state training institute, a senior officer introduced him in absentia by stating that his knowledge was limited beyond south of the Vindhyas but there was none in north of the Vindhyas who could beat Kanhaiyalal.'

'Clearly!' said Hemant. 'He was a man for all seasons! We shall never forget this, Papa. Each experience and person has a tale to tell and a message that can be useful in life.'

Shubhojit had enjoyed relating this story to his children. He could see that the communication between the three generations had gone a long way and fulfilled its role and purpose albeit unintended. Certain things were destined for a particular hour by the Almighty, thought Shubhojit, and should not be meddled with. Never could he have imagined that his son's wayward behaviour would be corrected by his grandmother's sagacious words, and that her simple tales of a bygone era would ignite a spark of yearning for one's forgotten antecedents.

Hemant and Neelakshi had lived with a rootless identity till now and had been groping in the dark for a meaningful existence. His separation from Yashodhra had made things more difficult for them. But now, they would be able to move ahead with a clear concept of the past and a firm knowledge of their lineage.

Shubhojit smiled, realizing that most of what he thought was perhaps true. And yet, his heart felt heavy once again.

He failed to understand the reason for his inward restlessness and overall sense of dismay. Power, Glory and Politics: these words no longer impressed him; and yet they were an integral part of his profession and life.

'Can I ever think of ignoring them or renouncing life if these are inseparable from reality? Can I opt for a life where such things don't exist or cease to matter? Is such a thought a mirage or a distant dream? Is it possible? After all, what is one's aim in life? What does a man want finally?'

Shubhojit looked around and found Kamladevi, Hemant and Neelakshi standing together on the terrace and enjoying the subtle beauty of the sunset and its radiance.

'Could this be the answer?' he wondered.

26

Shubhojit sat in a chair on the terrace. He was by himself: the family had wanted to do other things in the evening. A peculiar feeling of sadness overpowered him and he felt empty within. What was he thinking of? He wasn't sure. There came over him a strange stillness of spirit and a longing for inner peace.

The world, as he had seen it, was a terrible assortment of temptations, ambitions, excitement, allurements, passion and vanity. Man spent his life pursuing or grappling with them till nothing was left of his own self and he became a conglomeration of uncertainties, discontent and frustration. Entire mankind was engaged in these pursuits and suffered from the same malaise but still had to go its own way. Shubhojit had reached a stage where he did not envy anyone nor was he in a competition with anyone for anything. All he wanted now at the end of the day was quietude and a deep-rooted faith in himself.

He watched the clouded, crimson evening come to an end. He could see the faint outline of a rainbow; the sky looked majestic even with its dim but graceful presence.

'What a wonderful sight!' thought Shubhojit, admiring the beauty of nature and, suddenly, feeling somewhat pleased! He remembered the carefree days of his youth when he and his friends would watch a rainbow with great delight. It was a rare phenomenon and, therefore, much appreciated! The sight of a rainbow always awoke positive feelings in him; it seemed to give an assurance that the day's troubles would surely pass; it held out a promise of new beginnings. It could be considered a kind of symbol of God and His magnanimity; of the different colours present in nature and its vibrant wonders; and a perfect bonding between nature and the universe.

He saw the emergence of the rainbow at this particular moment as God's answer to his innermost turmoil; a call to break free of his mental demons and to rise above the mundane, seeking spiritual communion with the natural elements and the environment.

Bahadur came up with a fresh pot of tea: the first flush of Darjeeling green leaves, brewed only for a few minutes, served separately with sugar and milk. At times, Shubhojit liked to have tea without any sweetener or creamer. His penchant for certain things could appear to be very stylish; he was fond of good things and of the highest quality. He had a fierce streak of perfectionism that was reflected in his personality as well as all his actions, professional and personal.

Shubhojit sipped his tea, looking at the sky that was still tufted with ash-coloured clouds. He noticed the faint glimmer of the first star. The still atmosphere enthralled him. It was as if he were seducing the sacredness of solitude and heading towards ecstasy. It was a long time since he had felt so rooted in the moment, in his own home, and that was enough for now. He had, perhaps, been living his dream in reality.

'Mankind is mad,' thought Shubhojit, 'to run after material possessions and to fight over them. To be blind with jealousies and harbour an insatiable desire for acquisitions! And, in the process, ignoring the call of the soul. Men hanker after the immediacy of the moment, often forgetting that a mirage can last an entire lifespan and yet leave them unsatisfied. The call of the divine is lost in the glare of temporary allurements. A spiritual reawakening, therefore, is necessary to find out the truth of the cycle of life, death and rebirth. The time is ripe for these thoughts.'

The next morning, Shubhojit woke up and opened the window. It somehow eased his feeling of suffocation; he enjoyed looking at the vast expanse outside and basking in the warmth of the sunlight streaming into the room.

Each morning brought with it a wonderful spectacle: the pale yellow of the sun's rays ushering in moments of joy and hope for mankind; the carefree floating of the clouds; the blue sky reaching down to the horizon; all in harmony and yet each holding on to itself; the great dance of nature and the universe mesmerizing the world!

Shubhojit lay comfortably in his bed and watched the sun spread its warmth and light across the sky. For him, too, there had to be a new starting point somewhere; far from the madding crowds, in peaceful natural surroundings. He could sense his thoughts and emotions already heading in that direction.

Each day was like a new beginning for Shubhojit. As he recuperated quickly and steadily, his mind too raced ahead, from the past and the present towards the future. He was almost sure of the future he would like to have, but he could not erase past incidents and memories which had accompanied him to this point, almost close to the end of his career.

'A man, nay, an officer, is so naive,' thought Shubhojit, 'on the threshold of his professional life that it is impossible for him to believe that there could be alternative or subtle ways of dealing with a problem. All solutions or corrective measures need not necessarily be offensive. Youth may be wild, impatient and aggressive but, if I had thought carefully, I might have taken decisions which could be called mature or even politically correct. What would have been the harm in behaving with more patience, humility or maturity at that time?'

Shubhojit was amazed at the clarity of his memories. He thought back to his first posting as SDM (sub-divisional magistrate) and the first time he had sat in his courtroom. He was a novice as far as matters of administration were concerned. It was a small room: dark, damp and humid. The chairs, desks and tables which were kept there for the lawyers and the public, were rickety and undusted. His palms were moist and sweat broke out on his forehead, not because of the warm weather but out of nervousness and the uncertainty of impending situations.

'If I had known at that time,' thought Shubhojit, 'that my career would turn out so well, I wouldn't have been so jittery or nervous then.'

'But then you would have been complacent,' said his alter ego, 'and that would have been detrimental to your growth as an officer. It was your feeling of insecurity that made you work harder and carve out your path as a dedicated civil servant. You should appreciate your insecurities of that time as your greatest assets.'

Shubhojit found wisdom in this new perspective. 'Middle age is certainly like old wine: mature, with a better aroma, texture and mouthfeel.' He smiled as he remembered another incident that had disturbed him a lot at that time. It was during the elections, when he had asked a dignitary to leave the room because he was not supposed to be there. His conversation with Yashodhra about the incident was still fresh in his mind:

'Yashodhra, they are filing a writ petition against me in the high court.'

'Why?'

'I asked a person to leave my room because he was interfering in my administrative work during the counting of votes. He had no right to be present during the counting as he was not a representative of any party.'

'You did the right thing!'

'He was offended by my stiff, official behaviour and made it an ego issue.'

'Did you inform your Deputy Commissioner?'

'I did, and he told me that since I had asked this person to leave because he had no business being there, I had done the right thing!'

'These political people have big egos, dear. And they can go to any length when their egos are bruised and that, too, by a young SDM in his first posting.'

'This man is close to the important people of the district. He sent a written complaint to the chief secretary and even tried to bully his way through, boasting all the while of his proximity to the chief minister.'

'Did he succeed?'

'No way! The administrative machinery found out the facts and declared my handling of the situation in order and in compliance with the rules.'

'So, they chose to ignore his complaints.'

'Yes, and when those people didn't succeed, they decided to file a writ petition against me.'

'Let them! Will they succeed or get anything out of it?'

'They can, at the very least, harass the SDM and succeed in embarrassing him!'

'Don't take it that way! It is all a part of your job!'

'I don't really care! They can do what they want. They can't crush my spirit by indulging in these tactics while I am trying to uphold the rule of law. At the most, I shall have to appear in the court for clarification.'

'Take it in your stride, dear!'

'Oh, yes, my dear! With you by my side!'

Shubhojit had tried to appear calm before Yashodhra, as if he was not bothered by this unsavoury episode. But it had been easier said than done. Young and inexperienced as he was, he had spent sleepless nights mulling over its repercussions and impact on his professional life.

'Oh, God! I wish I had known at that time that their ill-will would not prevail and no blame would be attached to me,' thought Shubhojit. 'It would have saved me many anxious moments.'

Shubhojit was judging the incident from a mature point of view. Faced with a similar situation now, he would be a little more discreet; he would be careful and probably choose less offensive words. Instead of saying, 'Get out!' he would perhaps say, 'Maybe we could have a word later? I shall call you once the situation is under control', or something similar to that.

'A balanced manner of speech does not cost anything,' thought Shubhojit, 'but it can go a long way towards avoiding a confrontational situation and much hurt. But such thoughts and ideas come to one's mind with experience and age only.'

Yet another incident came to his mind. The employees

of a private chemical company had organised a large dharna outside the company premises due to non-payment of their salaries and other pending dues. They had virtually blockaded the place, with approximately forty trucks loaded with chemical gases and other substances parked inside. The managing director had vanished from the scene and become unavailable. Shubhojit toyed with the idea of taking the situation under his control; however, a senior officer happened to counsel him otherwise.

'First, it is the company's problem. Instruct your staff to trace the managing director and ask him to come to the negotiating table,' the deputy commissioner had advised him. 'Second, if this does not work out, then let the labour department of the state government come forward to defuse the situation and find a way out. If things still do not work out and the situation is likely to explode into a law-and-order problem, only then, take things under your control. But for that, let the company officials ask you for your help. Shubhojit, do not burn your fingers in the problems of other departments unless they specifically ask for your intervention and help.'

At that time, Shubhojit had been sceptical about the line of action suggested by his senior officer. Only now did he realize the appropriateness of taking such a stand. Young and impatient as he had been at that time, he would have immediately jumped into the fray and offered help on his own accord. Only now did he understand the wisdom of exercising restraint in tricky situations.

'Time, age and experience change one's outlook and behaviour, and usually for the better!' speculated Shubhojit. 'In any situation, one must exercise patience and weigh the pros and cons with a cool mind.' He remembered Sigmund Freud's oft-quoted saying, 'If youth knew; if age could.'

Shubhojit smiled. He felt he had done his best at that time. His reminiscences were providing him with rare glimpses and understanding into his past actions for which he had never found time earlier.

Everything, he supposed, had a time of its own.

27

SHUBHOJIT FOUND himself drawn more and more into his past life, personal as well as professional. He delved deep into memories and through layers of inner consciousness. The thought of office work had been relegated to the distant recesses of his mind which he visited only occasionally. Decisions taken under different circumstances were coming under the purview of his critical analysis, and he was judging them now along the parameters of time and hindsight.

Shubhojit's illness had been an eye-opener to him in many ways. He had been given an opportunity to view life from the other side of the fence. He was enjoying the unwonted moments of leisure, the intimacy with his family and the regimented eating and drinking. His unforeseen illness had warned him about the limitations of his body and he realized the fragility and transitoriness of life. A clear perception of the situation washed over him and he regarded it as divine enlightenment.

'Shall I get another chance in life?' he wondered. 'Shall I ever be able to undo or reverse the chain of events that my decisions have caused, whether personal or professional? Does anyone like me? Will people forget or forgive? Do I still have the ability to circumvent or control incidents or circumstances? Presumably, yes, if I try hard enough or with a sincere intent.'

Shubhojit's thought process ran unabated. A large part of his life still lay ahead of him. Except for missing Yashodhra's company, he had not been doing too badly on the personal front. His illness had cemented the bond with his children once again and also brought his mother in close touch with them. The bond among the three generations, dormant till now, stood strengthened, and he hoped fervently that it would continue to do so. Shubhojit greatly regretted the missing link. He heaved a deep sigh. 'Yashodhra! Oh, Yashodhra! Why did you? Couldn't you have had some more patience? Why the hell did you get carried away…? How could you have left me for someone so …?' Shubhojit was still unable to accept the reality.

'Of course, as far as my professional life is concerned, there have been far too many frustrating experiences,' thought Shubhojit. 'But they failed to dampen my spirit or affect my morale or change my resolve. I have always listened to the voice of my conscience and, to the best of my ability, tried to uphold the dignity attached to the office of a civil servant. I have never let the frustrating experiences get the better of me or dishearten me.'

Shubhojit looked up and saw that Hemant and Neelakshi had been watching him for some time, and were looking at each other meaningfully.

'What are you thinking, Papa?' asked Neelakshi, 'You seem lost in your memories.'

'Oh, nothing much, dear!'

'Do you think, Papa, you can fool us now?' coaxed Hemant. 'Why don't you tell us?'

'I was thinking of a particular incident,' said Shubhojit. 'I wonder whether it would interest you at all. I was a member of the electricity board of a state government.'

'What was the nature of your work and designation, Papa?' asked Neelakshi.

'I was looking after the financial and commercial aspects of the board's operations. I was posted there, after having served in an unimportant post for about a year, as a very senior colleague had a serious difference of opinion with the then-chairman,' said Shubhojit.

'Why were you serving in an unimportant office, Papa?'

'Well, many times, if you don't follow the "Yes, Sir" rule in the government, you are dubbed a defiant and non-cooperative officer, and you get side-lined into a posting where your nuisance value is minimal. This position, though important, was riddled with many problems and challenges. One had to deal with various situations, and either perform or face the wrath of one's superiors.'

'I am sure, Papa, it must have been very challenging!'

'Stimulating too,' said Shubhojit. 'It is only in adverse situations that one gets an opportunity to outperform others. I took it up as a new challenge.'

'Typical of you, Papa!' said Hemant. 'And now tell us the full story.'

Shubhojit smiled and tried to recollect the details of the incident. 'A special meeting had been convened,' he began, 'to deal with the financial crisis the utility was undergoing. The board had asked for government assistance. It was a peculiar and complex situation. The chairman of the electricity board was a former top officer and a real heavyweight. He was also a target of attack for those in position of power at the time. The trinity of the top state officers saw this as an opportunity to bring him down in the eyes of the chief minister, who was chairing the meeting. The main issue was management of funds for meeting with the utility's requirements to carry on its operations.'

Neelakshi asked, 'So, what happened then?'

'First,' said Shubhojit, 'we were given a long sermon about curtailing our expenditure. We were advised to take firm measures to reduce transmission and distribution losses, and to check theft of electricity which, of course, was widespread then, and continues to be so even now.'

'What is theft of electricity? Who does it?'

Shubhojit explained, 'A large number of consumers indulge in theft of electric power, thereby rendering the utility operations financially unviable. On top of it, the government decided to supply electricity to agricultural consumers at highly subsidized rates.'

'Why? Was that a good idea? Electricity tariffs should be based on the economic cost of supply of power to any sector,' said Hemant.

'Well, it is difficult to say if it was a good idea or not. But the operational losses caused by inefficient management practices is certainly most deplorable,' said Shubhojit.

'Please go on. Tell us what happened,' interjected Neelakshi.

'The finance secretary washed his hands off the whole affair, saying that the government could not spare funds for the power utility. We also learnt at this stage that a private finance company had approached the authorities, offering a large loan against a state government guarantee. A representative of the company happened to be present at the meeting. The main problem was the cost of funds,' said Shubhojit.

'What cost?'

'The cost would be 19.5 per cent as against the average cost of 14 per cent,' replied Shubhojit, 'and it was precisely that to which I objected. I argued that raising a loan on those terms, without any assured returns for repaying the loan, would have disastrous consequences for the utility.

'But, we were told that there was no alternative and the chief minister tried to justify the said loan on the pretext of sub-serving the public interest. Finding our backs to the wall, we insisted that this should be in the form of a government directive to the utility. At this stage, the finance secretary countered, "How can you even make such a proposal? The electricity board is an autonomous organization and the government cannot issue any such directions." I could not keep quiet any longer and retorted, "The electricity board is not autonomous, Sir, when it comes to determination of tariffs, it is not autonomous when it comes to appointment of staff, it is not autonomous when it comes to transfers and postings of its employees. How is it that its autonomy is conjured up only when it comes to taking responsibility?"'

'Oh God! You were way out of line there, Papa!' exclaimed Hemant.

'No, the chief minister's patience was commendable. He asked me why I was so adamant about not signing a letter of demand to the finance company. Left with no option, I decided to call a spade a spade. I told him, "Sir, I have barely rendered eleven years of service. But I am sure it is going to be a serious audit observation, and will call for pinpointing responsibility. I have no justification today. I shall have none after five years either. By that time, all these senior officers present here today would have retired with their pensions." Everybody was stunned, except one senior colleague who supported what I had said.'

'I am sure, Papa,' smiled Hemant, 'they did not take kindly to your response. They couldn't have taken it easy and forgiven you for saying that.'

'You are right, Hemant,' said Shubhojit. 'Everybody kept silent for a few moments. I could see their faces were all drawn with tension and unease. The chief minister seemed most annoyed. He looked at me for a few seconds and asked, "So you are not willing to issue a letter to the company for releasing the loan?"'

'"Sir, I shall happily do that but only when I am formally directed by the government to do so. I can't do it on my own authority. I am sorry, Sir!"'

'"All right!" said the chief minister and addressed the chief secretary, "You might as well transfer him out, and give him some other charge. Let another officer succeed him and do the needful. Put this decision on hold till then."'

'"Very well, Sir!" nodded the chief secretary.'

'Papa, how did you react to such a decision?' asked Neelakshi.

'I was greatly relieved,' said Shubhojit, 'and never regretted having taken the position that I did. Events, circumstances and situations can be very frustrating at times; and people non-cooperative and vindictive, but one has to hold on to one's convictions and take a principled stand even in tricky situations. This may seem hard in the beginning but saves one from getting into murky situations later.'

'Papa,' asked Neelakshi, 'have you ever lost your cool in any situation?'

'Oh, yes! Many times,' smiled Shubhojit. 'I shall tell you about this one incident. When I was deputy commissioner, there was one MLA—I forget his name—he would ring up at six o'clock in the morning every day and make a recommendation or two, often crossing the permissible lines.'

'Six in the morning? How awful!'

'Yes! I kept my cool for a few days initially and politely tried to point out to him the inappropriateness of his calling time and of the issues on which he was making recommendations. I told him gently that I would be in a better frame of mind to listen to recommendations while I was in the office. It would be easier for me to take action on those, if possible, in the office.'

'Did he understand?'

'No way! Either he was dense or trying to act smart. I lost my cool after about ten days and told him in no uncertain terms that his calls were not welcome the first thing in the morning. That he should have some consideration for the other person's convenience as well as some regard for his privacy. He was offended by my words, which he termed impudence and disrespect of a public man, and complained about my behaviour to the chief minister.'

'Really! Did anything come of it, Papa?'

'I think he was reprimanded by the chief minister who, though an iconic public man, always respected others' family time, unless there was an emergency. Also, he held good officers in high esteem and always stood by them.'

28

Quite early in his professional life, Shubhojit had learnt to hold on to his own value system in the complex world of bureaucracy. He had realized and internalized the fact that a man was accountable to his own self. If he wanted to remain true to himself and be happy, he did not need to bother about what others thought of him. He often said that he was never tensed or let those who do not listen to their conscience suffer from tensions. He had never been afraid of anyone or anything, except of confronting his deeper self in the mirror and feeling ashamed of his behaviour. He had done his best to prevent any unpalatable situation from rising; and if, by chance it did, his sanskars had always showed him the way. He did not fear the outside world and had always taken his own decisions, unmindful of public accolades or censure. He had been brought up to feel, react and respond in a particular way. He considered it his moral responsibility to adhere to it and to judge by it.

Memories of past experiences were coming back to him in flashes: unsavoury encounters with the administrative machinery; the prerogatives of political ascendancy; vendettas or judicial backlashes as a result of ego clashes. Shubhojit was going down memory lane and mulling over experiences with the authorities, detail by detail. It was like a nightmare or a learning experience, perhaps both. Since these incidents belonged to the past, and deserved only to be remembered, related and laughed at, it was easy for him to share them now with his children. He still felt uneasy, though, remembering the high degree of seriousness of many of them, and his own courage in taking unpopular decisions despite opposition from his colleagues and the authorities. At times, he had found himself at loggerheads with the system, on other occasions, his position had been that of a rudderless boat drifting all by itself in a fathomless sea against the wind. But he had been a part of it and he had been a hard nut to crack.

'Decisions taken in the past,' thought Shubhojit, 'with good intentions and with the public good in view can sometimes take an unexpected turn and go beyond one's control where one can only stand by, feeling helpless.' Hemant and Neelakshi were eager to know about the moments of frustration he had faced in his career. If he could share those experiences or incidents with them, it would give them some idea about how the systems worked in the country.

Eager to confide, he called out for his children and his mother. Kamladevi, too, must listen to this and judge it in the scales of her rustic wisdom. Though illiterate, she had a sufficient understanding of the ways of the world and a method of looking at life that was different from that of others. She would be interested in hearing what he wanted to share with his children. Hemant and Neelakshi came immediately and seemed as interested as ever. So was Kamladevi.

'Hemant, Neelu,' said Shubhojit, 'I want to tell you about an experience, call it weird, call it exasperating, where I did not or could not understand what to do or undo the chain of events that had been set in motion but with the best of intentions.'

'Oh, do tell!' was the prompt reply.

'This goes back to the time when I was in charge of the

State Industrial Development Corporation. We were set to proceed with the hitherto largest acquisition of land in the state for the development of an industrial township, expected to attract a huge investment and create large-scale employment opportunities.'

'When the government acquires privately owned land, it is supposed to pay compensation for it, right?' asked Hemant.

'Yes, of course, it has to,' said Shubhojit. 'I am coming to that. Except for land situated within a band of about two to three acres from the national highway, the actual price of land in the market was about ₹3 lakh per acre. The district collector had fixed an all-inclusive price varying between ₹2.75 lakh and ₹3.15 lakh. As for the land adjoining the national highway, it was fixed at about ₹6.50 lakh. Just before the announcement of the award, I had made the necessary inquiries, and I pleaded with the district collector to raise the price of the entire land to ₹6.50 lakh. The district collector warned me of the financial implications, but my proposal to pay a higher compensation to the landowners-farmers was driven by the best intentions. I wanted them to benefit from the acquisition of their land by the government, and I wanted to improve their financial status. A good compensatory amount would enable them to acquire agricultural land elsewhere, and if not more, at least equal to what they had lost. Initially, the farmers seemed pleased and, on the very first day, came forward to accept 50 per cent of the amount.'

'Initially, you say?' asked Neelakshi. 'There seems to be a twist in the story.'

'Yes, there is,' said Shubhojit, 'and the twist was brought about by some of our worthy lawyers who are always in search of clients, and of whom a special breed has emerged at the district level. They specialize in filing references for enhancement of land compensation. They are very good at convincing farmers about the likely benefits of contesting a proposed compensation. As fees, they charge a percentage of the enhancement ordered at the district level.'

'I am sure, Papa,' said Hemant, 'that the lawyers must have wheedled the poor farmers. And when was this?'

'Of course they did, Hemant,' said Shubhojit. 'The acquisition proceedings were initiated in 1994 and the award was announced in March 1997. The references were filed soon thereafter and the district court enhanced the amount to about ₹8 lakh per acre.'

'Oh my God!'

'But, that is not the full story,' said Shubhojit. 'This was still within the acceptable range. An appeal was filed in the high court, where it was further increased to about ₹15 lakh. And mind you, that was only the basic market price. Add to that a solatium and the interest thereon with effect from 1994.

'Then, the State Corporation preferred an appeal in the Supreme Court, which initially directed that the amount be paid at the rate of ₹10 lakh per acre and that the final outcome be awaited. The matter was finally decided in 2010, and the compensation amount was determined at ₹20 lakh per acre on the basis of one managed transaction involving only about 500 square yards.'

'Papa!' Hemant and Neelakshi's eyes went wide with disbelief. 'It is unbelievable!'

'Yes! But true,' Shubhojit continued, 'and this amount was to be reckoned as the basic market price as of April 1994. A solatium at 30 per cent was to be calculated on this amount. Further, interest at 15 per cent was payable on the basic price and on the solatium amount for a period of sixteen years.'

'What is solatium?'

'It is the compensation paid by the government for the compulsory acquisition of land,' Shubhojit explained.

'It must have worked out to a huge amount,' said Neelakshi.

'Well, unbelievable as it may appear, the gross amount of compensation worked out to around ₹90 lakh per acre.'

'₹90 lakh!' exclaimed Hemant. 'How grossly unfair to the government and the corporation! How did they manage to pay?'

'The corporation filed more than 250 reviews in more than 250 cases, which were heard but dismissed with costs, almost with a vengeance,' continued Shubhojit. 'They had to think of quick ways to deal with this problem. While the enhanced amount could be recovered from the plot allottees, the entrepreneurs needed some lead time. As such, the corporation had to raise a huge loan from the banks to pay the enhanced compensation amount.'

'Was that the end of the story?'

'By no means, it was only the beginning. The district courts started using the Supreme Court determined rate as the basic rate for land acquisition with 1994 as the base year. This principle was applied by the district courts to all other acquisitions in the area after 1994 and the base rate was updated with an increase of 12 per cent every year,' said Shubhojit.

'The industrial corporation must have gone bankrupt!' said Hemant. 'How did it manage?'

'Well, it almost went bankrupt.' Shubhojit heaved a sigh. 'The financial crunch was so severe that the industrial corporation had to raise huge loans for meeting with its obligations, which were largely a creation of the courts.

The cash flows of a once-vibrant organization were virtually brought to a standstill.'

'Papa,' said Hemant, 'now I understand what you meant when you said that even a well-intentioned decision can take an ugly turn in due course of time, not envisaged at the time of the decision.'

'Yes, it is very frustrating,' said Shubhojit, 'that most of the time our judicial system does not recognize the consequences of its decisions. Heightened egos often ignore the larger interests, and unfairly so. Our adjudication system is so expensive that it has no place for the common man.

'There are many, many instances where one has been frustrated by the courts. A road project for a few kilometres can be held up for years due to a stay on the acquisition of a small portion of land forming a critical front. However much one may plead regarding its criticality, entreaties have often been met with stiff resistance. The worst part is that they refuse to give the officer a hearing. Only a lawyer is allowed to plead before them.' Shubhojit sounded angry and helpless.

'Can't a PIL be filed against their decisions?' asked Neelakshi.

'PILs are not entertained when they challenge actions taken or not taken by brother judges!' said Shubhojit. 'These are the ways of the world, and one can only feel totally helpless and depressed, and wring one's hands in desperation. I have often felt pushed into a corner in certain situations without having the option to quit or initiate changes in something that is apparently beyond control.'

'Papa,' asked Neelakshi, 'did you ever feel that you were in the wrong service? If you were given the choice once again, would you still opt for it?'

'Oh, yes, my dear, I would still go for it,' said Shubhojit, most emphatically. 'The service has given me ample opportunities to do my little bit for the larger public good. At times, when one feels bogged down by immense pressures from various quarters, one may feel like giving up, but it is still worth it. Given the little space one enjoys in the work arena, one can still make a difference in the system by initiating many changes or at least starting the process of change. This might be the USP of our service. I may share some other instances with you. Maybe tomorrow, children, I am feeling a little tired now.'

Kamladevi had been listening intently to the conversation between father and children, and enjoying getting a first-hand account of the working of the government and the administrative system. She only remarked, 'Son, God has been generous in entrusting judges with the responsibility of rendering justice. They should see for themselves whether they are only deciding cases or delivering justice.'

She was at a stage of life where nothing came as a surprise or shock to her. Stoicism had always been a part of the mental make-up of the members of her generation where the values imbibed by them during childhood had always stood them in good stead when they ran into rough weather. They had never felt like hanging up their boots and saying goodbye to life. They would rather face, confront and combat the acid test of life and emerge victorious with a smile on their faces.

Such was their resolve, tenacity and determination to move ahead! Kamladevi looked at her progeny and smiled widely. She could afford to do that now!

29

Talking for the first time at home about the knotty situations he had encountered at his workplace had had a cathartic effect on Shubhojit's mind. He wished that he had done it earlier. He had never bared his heart to Yashodhra in this manner. He had never cared to make time or create an opportunity to do so. Nor had he wanted to. He had never shared his anxieties with his wife lest they unnecessarily upset her. But he was wrong or had been proved to be so. His silence before Yashodhra had resulted in a widening of the gulf that had crept into their relationship. Lack of communication due to lack of time had resulted in a souring of relations till they reached a dead end. After that, it had been a downhill journey.

If only he had taken serious note of the early signs and made amends! An occasional, heart-to-heart talk with his wife would have saved the failing marriage. The tragic marital experience had shown him that what a woman wanted the most, out of all things in the world, was to be loved. A well-loved woman rarely betrays her man. But, if she feels neglected or left out in the cold, she might go to any lengths to sever her ties with the man, even if it were the husband.

This realization had come rather too late in his life. But God had given him this unexpected opportunity to build a new relationship with his children. Sharing his innermost thoughts and work experiences had brought him much closer to Hemant and Neelakshi, and even to his mother. The dormant bond had been revived; his children had once again started feeling themselves as an integral part of a family; his mother's concerns had been put to rest and he, himself, felt lighter and cured of his repressed inner self. It had also brought Yashodhra back into their lives, if only in the form of a mention of a name or occasional visits to inquire about his health. Though a remote possibility, life could be looking up once again!

Shubhojit remembered that he hadn't ended the story he had been telling them the previous day. The loose ends still needed to be tied up. They were an eye-opener for Hemant and Neelakshi. Having led a sheltered and privileged life as the children of a high-ranking official, they had never come across such incidents or cared to know how the normal world functioned. They had never felt the need to do so. But a brush with the uncertainties of life had convinced Shubhojit to prepare his children to face the challenges they might confront in real life. He was happy to note that Hemant and Neelakshi had been as eager to know and learn about these things as he had been to tell them. Kamladevi, on her part, had been a support, as always.

The door opened and Hemant and Neelakshi walked in. They made a lovely pair of siblings who enjoyed hanging out with each other. As Shubhojit was recovering quickly and feeling almost back to normal, their confidence, too, was being restored. They were no longer dejected or suffering from anxiety and uncertainty. That had been replaced by a renewed faith in their own selves and capabilities. They had listened attentively to all that their grandmother and father had to tell them, and they had gained a fresh perspective on life. Shubhojit addressed them directly: 'Come on, Neelakshi,

Hemant, I have to complete the details of the incident I was relating yesterday.'

'That is good, Papa!' answered Neelakshi. 'You remembered on your own this time.'

'Generally, I don't forget!' said Shubhojit. 'It is only that I have had some spare time and your undivided attention.'

'You wanted to tell us more about it, Papa?' asked Hemant.

'I told you about the government policy of acquiring land in the public interest,' said Shubhojit, 'and then paying adequate compensation to the interested persons. Also, how the matter can take a U-turn if the courts choose to interfere. Sometimes, people make a request that their land be acquired.'

Hemant asked, 'Request the government to acquire their land?'

'Yes, in areas where the government-determined compensation amount is higher than the price they would be able to fetch in the open market. Another attraction is a host of accompanying benefits,' said Shubhojit. 'Who can pass up a chance to make a quick buck? People no longer hesitate to beat the system if it can get them some additional money. I have seen a few people undertaking plantation in their fields during the acquisition proceedings.'

'To what purpose?'

'Under the mistaken belief that they would be entitled to an additional amount against the value of the trees planted by them,' Shubhojit smiled.

'The world is full of strange people and happenings, Papa.'

'Yes! Initially, opposition to government takeover of land was in those areas where people thought they would get a better price in the open market compared with what the government was offering. They would find various reasons and arguments seeking exclusion of their land from acquisition. Overnight, they would construct samadhis of their ancestors, spread out over a large area, to get the land exempted.

'Did the authorities ever relent in any such cases, Papa?'

'Yes, of course!' replied Shubhojit. 'Exceptions can always be made in deserving cases, wherever possible. Let me tell you about the case of a seventy-five-year-old distressed man who came to me with a request. His family had seventeen acres of land that had come under acquisition about twenty years earlier. They had accepted the acquisition and relocated to another place where they bought twenty-five acres of agricultural land. To their bad luck, this land too came under acquisition. The family was disturbed at the thought of having to relocate.'

'What did you do?'

'The old man had three surviving sons and eight grandsons. He had come with three of his sons and one grandson, the one whose father had expired. He said that they had built their house in a corner of the field, but had no objection to the acquisition of their land, and had already accepted the compensation amount. His only request was that one acre, on which their existing house was located, be exempted. They needed to carve out at least eight plots out of that one acre so that each of his grandsons could construct his house thereon and they would not have to relocate. He wanted nothing more.'

'Did you accommodate him?'

'Yes, I could not have found a more genuine case; he was truthful, straight and honest. In his presence, I issued an order for the release of this one acre of his land. The old man had tears in his eyes and merely said, "I had heard about you. Today, I have seen for myself. Thank you and God bless you!" I was equally happy since I had done justice to a deserving man.'

'The government is a complex entity, Papa,' said Hemant. 'It has wide-ranging powers to help, govern as well as destroy. It can suit, accommodate or mar anybody's or everybody's interests, isn't it so?'

'Who has known it better than me?' sighed Shubhojit. 'As a matter of interest, some disgruntled persons, whom I had not been able to oblige, filed a complaint against me alleging that I had released that man's land for a financial consideration. It was very gratifying to receive a call from him that he would always be willing to vouch for me.'

'That was good!' exclaimed Kamladevi.

'It is a well-known fact that some government servants do indulge in undesirable practices but, as long as one has honesty of purpose, people generally respect you. And one has to be open to meeting with people and talking things out with them! However, there are large numbers who opt for accusatory postures,' continued Shubhojit.

'Really, Papa? I suppose the public believes in giving only brickbats to the government. It rarely appreciates the good measures taken.'

'You may be right but let me tell you that good deeds don't always go unrecognized. I have always maintained that a large part of the problem is over when you place yourself in the shoes of the aggrieved and then think of a solution. When you acquire land for any urbanization-related activity, contiguity of land is a critical requirement for efficient planning and provision of all civic services. It happens sometimes that the entire land of a village, except the actual *abadi* or populated area, is acquired. Now, one has to appreciate that animal husbandry is an inseparable part of village life. Besides, the villagers also need land for their expanding families. We carried out an experiment in consultation with the local residents of a particular village. Having acquired every inch of its land next to the abadi area, we planned residential plots as well as plots of land for their common needs and their animals, in contiguity. The area was then surrounded by a twenty-metre-wide green belt planted with two rows of trees. Barring a few disgruntled persons, almost everyone in the village appreciated this initiative. Environmentally too, it was a win-win situation for both sides.'

'Was the government planning to build an industrial township on it, Papa?' Hemant's tone was mischievous.

'Well, whatever the government wanted to use it for!' smiled Shubhojit.

'But wouldn't that be environmentally bad?'

'That's an altogether separate issue,' smiled Shubhojit. 'You are trespassing into a forbidden area. There is a continuous heated debate between environmentalists and the industry-promoters. Neither appreciates the other's viewpoint. They go on with their cat-and-dog fights to the disadvantage of both.'

'Whom do you promote, Papa? In whose philosophy do you actually believe?' asked Neelakshi earnestly.

'I don't think that either should grow or survive at the other's cost. In fact, it is not a matter of either of the two. Industrial activity is necessary for economic growth but not by damaging the environment. Economic growth has to follow the principles of sustainability. How would we live if we spoil the quality of the air that we breathe? What would we drink if we pollute the water? We can't sacrifice our future for short-term gains,' replied Shubhojit.

'But they present such conflicting scenarios! How do you

reconcile the two opposing factions?' asked Neelakshi.

'You are asking me? I have held these two responsibilities simultaneously. Things can be difficult and there are challenges but all these issues can be settled if you have clarity of vision and determination. Problems come up only when your actions are driven by an agenda,' said Shubhojit.

'How long did you last with both the charges?'

'Well, not very long,' Shubhojit laughed aloud. 'It was becoming too much and I requested to be relieved of at least one. And I was obliged.'

'Did you regret it?'

'No way!' said Shubhojit. 'There is no scope for regret in the service. There is only policymaking and action…good or bad, only time can tell.'

30

For the last few days, Shubhojit and his family had been talking only of the past and past events. Yet, Shubhojit felt his past slipping away from his fingers. He had been reliving his youth and its interesting happenings with a passion he thought he had lost. But the chain of events in the immediate past had forced him to look back on the chequered career that he had nourished with his time and sweat. He had thoroughly enjoyed his innings and felt proud of most of the professional decisions he had taken, sometimes, despite dissent. So much so that he felt that he had reached the end of his patience level and was mentally ready to take a sabbatical any time now.

But sharing and discussing his experiences with his children had helped...helped him de-stress. To some extent, it had also taken the edge off his anger, eased the frustrations and the resentments. In the past, he had never enjoyed being with his children as much he was doing now. But, the present too, seemed to be slipping away from his grip, and he was becoming increasingly aware of its momentariness. He knew that his children and mother would soon be leaving for their respective destinations. Hemant had overstayed his vacation and so had Neelakshi. If he wanted to share something more with them, he still had the opportunity, but time was running out.

'It has been so different,' thought Shubhojit, 'talking to the children now that they are all grown up and have the ability to understand. It has been like a conversation between adults, without pretensions or formalities. It has been truly a reciprocal communication between us, with each being appreciative of the other's point of view. The bitter memories of the unhappy past have been washed away by this new-found companionship of the three generations.'

It had become almost a habit for Hemant and Neelakshi to come to their father's bedroom first thing in the morning. All three looked forward to this meeting. As they entered the room, Shubhojit greeted them warmly. 'Aren't you guys late today? Where is your grandmother? Help her come in.'

They saw Kamladevi trying to push open the door with her stick, and immediately rose to help her come forward. The happy quartet sat down and smiled warmly at each other. Familiar times were back!

'Neelakshi,' said Shubhojit, 'you asked me once about the frustrating experiences in my long career as a civil servant. Today, I shall tell you about one.'

'Do you still see them as frustrating, Papa?' asked Hemant.

'To some extent, yes!' said Shubhojit. 'Though I wanted to learn and make improvements to the extent that I could, I always felt restricted by the predefined rules and regulations. My long stint in government service has convinced me that the processes and the procedures were considered more important than the final outcome.'

'Would you call that red tape, Papa?' asked Neelakshi.

'Perhaps, yes!' said Shubhojit. 'And that's how the "civil service" became "the bureaucracy". For instance, procurement involves men, material and services. Even if a small stationery item is needed in the office, there is such an elaborate procedure that the whole exercise seems a waste of manpower and resources. First, the office staff may not always be competent enough to draw up a tender document, lay down the specifications and draft an advertisement in the newspapers, and then give the whole procedure a time frame of at least three weeks. Apart from all this, there is the process of evaluating the bids, pinpointing the lowest bidder and then, finally, awarding the tender. This process has to be followed for each and every item that is to be procured. You can imagine the amount of time wasted and the involvement of a number of people.'

'Would you say, Papa,' asked Hemant, 'that these processes are irrelevant and should be done away with?'

'Not necessarily!' answered Shubhojit. 'I shall relate one instance to you. One morning, at the peak of the summer season, one of the transformers in my office building broke down. The heat was so severe that it was almost impossible for my staff to continue working in the building. I was furious when I was informed that the spare transformer had been lying unused on account of some fault. Nobody had taken steps to get it repaired. It was an emergency situation. Following the prescribed processes and procedures for getting it repaired or replaced would have taken us through a major part of the summer. I got in touch with the power utility, called for a transformer from their stocks and put in a request to the accounts department for its payment. I put all the facts in black and white on the relevant file so that nobody could raise a finger against the decision I had taken. Sometimes, one has to have the guts to override time-consuming processes and take a decision.'

'That still doesn't answer my question, Papa?' asked Hemant.

'Well, I wouldn't say that the processes are irrelevant and should be done away with,' said Shubhojit, 'because they function best as checks and balances. Not everyone spends public money as prudently as he would spend his own. In the absence of a system, greed or negligence might result in chaotic situations. Of course, a system too is liable to be abused and if we were to divest it of the procedural ingredient, it would go totally haywire. Now, does that answer your question, Hemant?'

'Oh, yes, it does!' said Hemant. 'But so much time is wasted in useless and unproductive work!'

'Yes, it is,' said Shubhojit, 'but that too can be taken care of. Most government departments have developed their own systems to address these day-to-day problems...'

'What does that mean?'

'For example, I may decide to outsource the operation and management of all my office electrical works. They apply a professional ecosystem to the whole procedure and prevent the department from wasting its time over these things. The process gets speeded and taken care of efficiently, and the office staff doesn't end up doing something at which they are not adept,' explained Shubhojit.

'That doesn't sound too bad?'

'Yes, not bad at all,' said Shubhojit, 'except that, at times, things can be unsatisfactory on various grounds. One can become a prisoner of the system anywhere, anyhow. And the man who doesn't toe the line is often lost and left to defend himself and his actions.'

'I think we understand what you mean, Papa!' said Hemant.

'I hope you do!' smiled Shubhojit. 'Who knows? You might be a part of this system in future. And you might be prepared to deal with it better than I have been, perhaps.'

'Why do you say that, Papa?' asked Neelakshi.

'There was nobody to tell me about these things and in such a candid manner,' smiled Shubhojit. 'I had to learn the hard way, to carve out an identity on my own terms. I faltered many times; got embroiled in tricky situations; was often mocked at; even made a scapegoat at times; was shunted around aimlessly for long periods. But, thank God! I came out of it all, unscathed and still more determined to follow my own path.'

'Well, we are your children, Papa,' said Hemant. 'We shall definitely carry on your legacy and follow the example you have set for others to follow. We shall always try to uphold the family values too.'

"Yes, Papa, you can depend on us, always,' said Neelakshi.

'Now, don't get overly sentimental about these matters. Let things happen in their normal course, and follow your instincts. They never go wrong, they are like a beacon of light in adverse circumstances, and they show the way. Your own good judgement will always see you through in life. Don't worry, love!' Shubhojit himself seemed to be getting emotional. 'Now, Hemant, I suppose your extended holiday is coming to an end. What is your plan of action?'

'Papa! I don't want to leave you at this point in time.' Hemant, too, seemed overwhelmed by his emotions. 'We have gained, unexpectedly, an insight into your illustrious career and your personality. We had never cared to learn about it when we were young. We took everything for granted till things fell apart and we were left shaken and confused.'

'Most of all,' said Neelakshi, 'we have enjoyed listening to our grandmother and getting to know about the roots from which we come. It has been a real eye-opener for us, and a pleasant one, indeed! Both of us now feel so connected with the family, Papa!'

'Have you been in touch with your mother lately, Hemant?' asked Shubhojit. 'I was wondering about her well-being. I am sure she would like to see you before you leave for your college, right?'

Shubhojit made a vain attempt to hide his wish to see Yashodhra. It's been a long while, he thought, since I last saw her. Hemant and Neelakshi looked at each other and smiled.

Shubhojit, though quick to notice, avoided their glance; instead, he poured himself a glass of water and drank it. In order to ward off his embarrassment, he asked Kamladevi, 'Ma, would you like to have a cup of tea?'

'Can I get a cup of coffee, instead?' asked Kamladevi.

Hemant and Neelakshi burst out laughing. 'Grandma! We have spoiled you, haven't we?'

'Do I stand spoiled on account of merely asking for coffee?' Kamladevi laughed. 'I have seen things which can be called modern even by your own standards. I can still think more original than you people combined together. I am the eldest as well as the oldest of the generation.'

Shubhojit loved the light tone and the path the conversation had taken, making the atmosphere pleasant and jovial. 'Now, who will order the coffee?'

'Papa, I'll just go down and order a few things,' said Neelakshi, 'since Hemant will be leaving tomorrow evening. Mom is dropping in, in a short while, to meet with him. We can all sit together and have pakoras and coffee...'

'Like old times!' said Hemant and looked at Shubhojit, who did not miss the irony of the statement. But he felt light-hearted and relaxed. The enforced rest had brought him a much-needed respite from routine and a change in perspective. As also, a realization of the fleeting moments and of life itself!

While Neelakshi was downstairs, instructing Bahadur, the doorbell rang and Yashodhra came in, carrying a few parcels. Mother and daughter hugged each other and went upstairs to meet the rest of the family. Hemant was overjoyed and so was Shubhojit, though a little more restrained. Kamladevi, too, acknowledged her with a smile and raised her hands to bless her.

'Mom!' said Hemant. 'I knew you would come today! How nice to have you here!'

'Why wouldn't I come, my dear?' smiled Yashodhra. 'I know you are leaving tomorrow. Now, get prepared to listen to a long list of instructions. Would you mind that?'

'Do I have an option, Mom?' asked Hemant with a mischievous glint in his eyes. 'They have been my companion since childhood. Every word of yours has been like law in the house or, at least, you made it seem like one. Didn't we always listen to you?'

'Okay, enough of that!' said Yashodhra. 'Hemant, you have to be very serious about your studies since this is your final year of college. Your marks and rank will go a long way in determining your career. I am sure you realize it only too well. And you have to supplement the hostel food with extra nutrition. I have made some besan laddoos for you and Neelakshi. Keep them safe in your locker and eat at least one at breakfast along with a glass of milk. This will keep you satisfied till lunchtime. I hope you are carrying some light woollens.'

'Oh, Mom, please!' laughed Hemant and hugged her warmly.

'Neelakshi! Are we getting coffee?' asked Kamladevi.

Just then, Bahadur opened the door and brought in a large tray with steaming-hot coffee and cheese sandwiches. While Hemant helped him lay things on the table, Bahadur looked at Shubhojit, smiled and said, 'Sir, these are not for you. I have made vegetable sandwiches for you and you will eat only those. But, you are allowed freshly made coffee, frothy and milky.'

Loud cheers went up from all of them and Bahadur was given a pat on the back by Kamladevi! Bahadur winked at Hemant and ran downstairs.

31

A NEW day dawned, bringing with it an element of uncertainty in Shubhojit's household. There was a touch of sadness in the air despite the attempts of the four family members to make light of the impending separation. As the minutes ticked by, the level of tension rose, which none of them was ready to acknowledge or confront. It was writ large on their faces and their body language confirmed it.

There was an unaccustomed listlessness in Kamladevi's demeanour as she walked about the house aimlessly; Neelakshi's face bore a downcast look, and Shubhojit tried hard to appear normal and to control his emotional flux. They were all slowly coming to terms with the reality of Hemant's departure. Hemant, aware of his family's feelings, busied himself in gathering his belongings and packing them. Intensity of sentiments had always disconcerted him; he had not learnt to deal with them. His mother's absence at such moments only added to his tension.

Hemant's flight was scheduled to leave in a few hours. This meant that they still had time to have breakfast together one last time before parting. They wondered when they would all be together under the same roof again and for such a long time.

Keeping in mind the significance of the moment, and with a lot of affection, Bahadur had prepared a lavish breakfast. A meal together, he thought, might help ease the stressful moments for the family. He had taken special care to cater to the varied tastes of all the family members: there were aloo paranthas with green chutney, cheese patties, poha and vegetable sandwiches, along with cold milk, sweet and salted buttermilk, tea and coffee. Kamladevi wore a wide smile on her face; she was the most stoic of them all and took things in her stride. Shubhojit felt a sense of loss and toyed with the food; Neelakshi sat gloomy, trying to hold back her tears. Bahadur ran in and out of the kitchen, placing various things on the table and trying in vain to cheer them up.

Time was running out and they had to hurry through their breakfast. This meal was so different from the ones they had been having for the past few days. The last month had been like a voyage of discovery for the family, with each member getting to know each other, more intimately than ever before. Although it had started inauspiciously with Shubhojit unexpectedly falling ill, it had changed their outlook and forced them to take a closer look at each other and at themselves.

The low-spirited meal over, it was time for Hemant to take leave of his father and grandmother. Neelakshi had insisted on accompanying him to the airport. Hemant touched his grandmother's feet and hugged his father.

'Papa, promise me that you will take care of your health and take the prescribed precautions. You can't afford to be casual in your approach.'

'Of course, I shall! Don't worry on that account. Take your studies seriously and make your mark in whatever you do. This is the time for you to take your own decisions. Don't waste your time! It will never come back. Grow up, my dear boy!' Shubhojit tightened his embrace.

'I shall, Papa! I have learnt a lot during the last one month and I have understood the importance of things I had ignored earlier. You will never again have to hear a complaint about me. You are my role model and I do want to follow in your footsteps.' Hemant's spontaneous response brought cheer to Shubhojit's face. The bond between them had grown stronger since his illness and he didn't want the intensity to fade away in the near future.

'Neelakshi,' said Hemant, 'you are closer to home and so will be able to keep an eye on Papa. Don't let him neglect his health.'

'Don't let that worry you, dear bro! You just concentrate on your studies,' smiled Neelakshi.

Kamladevi had been watching them with a sense of total satisfaction. Nothing else could have given her more pleasure. The sinking of difference of opinion between Shubhojit and his children was a positive step in their relationship. She considered it a divine blessing that all of them were together and in good health. She had been toying with the idea of going back to the village for a while and returning after some time, perhaps. She had been away for a long time from her home and had started missing the company of her friends and their uninhibited gossip and laughter. She was satisfied that Shubhojit was recuperating quickly. Sooner or later, he, too, would be resuming work and would not need her at home. She decided to broach the subject with him after Hemant and Neelakshi had gone their own ways.

Bahadur had kept the luggage in the car and came inside to inform them. The dreaded moment was finally here. They all came out to bid Hemant goodbye, with Neelakshi ushering him on. A quiet and intimate hug with the father and the grandmother did away with the need for further words.

Neelakshi prodded him on: 'Get in quickly, Hemant! We are getting late.'

Hemant opened the door, got in and waved fervently at his father, as the car started moving.

'Take care, son!' smiled Shubhojit.

'Take good care of yourself, old man, and of your mother too!' laughed Hemant.

The car slowly moved out of the gate and sped towards its destination. Kamladevi and Shubhojit stood on the porch for a few moments. The fact that the children had gone was taking time to register and be accepted. Neelakshi, of course, would be coming back after seeing Hemant off, but she, too, would leave soon, in pursuit of her career. The pleasant family reunion was almost over, with things falling in their right place. Kamladevi looked at Shubhojit, patted him on the back and said, 'It is time for me to go, Shubho!'

'Go where, Ma?' Shubhojit pretended not to understand her.

'I have been away from the village for a while now. You are much better now and will soon be returning to your work. Make arrangements for my return in a couple of days or so.'

'You, too, Ma! Why don't you stay for a little while more?'

The prospect of being left alone once again saddened Shubhojit. How much he wished he could postpone it somehow!

'All right, Ma,' said Shubhojit, 'let Neelakshi come back. My check-up is due tomorrow. We shall take a final call on things after that.'

The next day, Shubhojit went for his medical check-up. Dietary precautions, a relaxed lifestyle, absence of stress and the family reunion had all had a salutary influence on his mind and calmed his nerves. Coming face to face with family issues and resolving them amicably had resulted in a renewed optimism and raised his sagging morale. Shubhojit and his family had been able to steer their way successfully through the stressful, tricky web of family issues and relationships. He had realized that life was too precious and short to let it get bogged down in mundane technicalities and unproductive, time-consuming ordeals that did nothing to provide nourishment to the soul. An unconscious severing with one's roots can only add to the feelings of discontentment, he thought. Shubhojit was determined to live the rest of his life on his own terms, irrespective of societal and professional pressures or obligations.

The visit to the hospital with Neelakshi in the morning turned out to be a routine affair. All his tests were clear and he was declared fit and able to lead a normal life. He was prescribed medicines for three months and given a list of instructions for a disciplined routine of a controlled diet, plenty of leisure time and exercise.

'We would love to meet you, Sir,' said the doctor, 'and keep in touch but not in the hospital. This is not the right place for you. You still have a lot to accomplish in life. Take care of your health, Sir!'

Shubhojit smiled at the warm words and Neelakshi folded her hands in gratitude.

They returned home and found Yashodhra waiting for them and chatting warmly with Kamladevi. The awkwardness between the two women seemed to have melted away during the past few weeks. A common desire for Shubhojit's and the children's welfare had brought them together and helped to bury the hatchet. The two women had reached a level of truce, where it was possible to go beyond the personal domain and think about the interests of the family alone.

'Hi, Mom!' said Neelakshi hugging her. 'There is good news for all of us. Papa is absolutely fine and can start going to office whenever he wants. He just has to be careful.'

Neelakshi's words had the desired effect on Kamladevi and Yashodhra. Both were visibly happy. Kamladevi raised her hands towards the sky and thanked God profusely. Yashodhra chose to be more restrained in her response.

'Be careful, Shubhojit, and don't neglect your health,' was all she said.

'Don't worry, Yashodhra!'

'Neelakshi!' Yashodhra turned her eyes towards her 'What is your plan now? It is time for you, too, to get back to your studies. Isn't it?'

'Yes, Mom! You are right. I shall be getting back to my old routine.'

'I can drop you back at your Nani's. Tell me when you are ready.' Yashodhra looked at Shubhojit.

'Well,' said Shubhojit, 'we wouldn't want to detain her any longer. She has been here long enough. But, Neelakshi, I would like to see you more often.'

'Yes, Papa! I shall not give you a chance to complain in this regard,' said Neelakshi. She then addressed Yashodhra, 'Mom, give me some time. My bag is all packed and I shall be down with you in a short while.'

'We can have coffee and snacks in the meanwhile,' suggested Kamladevi.

'Oh, yes! Why not?' smiled Yashodhra and rose to go to the kitchen and give the necessary instructions to Bahadur.

Shubhojit realized that it would perhaps be a long time before Yashodhra, his mother, Neelakshi and he would next have a cup of coffee together and enjoy a family get-together. He wondered when they would meet again and whether Yashodhra would be able to make such frequent visits, even to inquire about his health. He heaved a deep sigh and Yashodhra looked at him, making an effort to read his thoughts. It was hard for her to keep up the pretence of not understanding what was going on in Shubhojit's mind.

Kamladevi chose to be a mute spectator and waited for either Bahadur or Neelakshi to arrive and ease the awkward moment.

'Yashodhra,' said Shubhojit trying to sound calm, 'do visit whenever the children come to stay.'

'Oh, yes, of course!' replied Yashodhra. 'I shall certainly come.'

Just then, Bahadur appeared, carrying a large tray, laden with snacks and cups of steaming-hot coffee.

'Neelakshi, come quickly,' Yashodhra called out loudly, 'the snacks are getting cold.'

Neelakshi appeared a few moments later, carrying a big suitcase and two small bags. 'I am ready, Mom!'

'Come and sit beside me, dear,' said Kamladevi, 'and hand me a cup of coffee.'

'Eat a few snacks first, Dadima,' smiled Neelakshi, 'I know you love them!'

'Neelakshi,' said Kamladevi, 'when you come again, do call me as well. I would very much like to be here.'

'Certainly, Dadima! We shall all get together regularly from now on.'

It was time for Yashodhra and Neelakshi to take leave. As

Shubhojit and Kamladevi saw them off, she told her son, 'It is my turn to go now, Shubhojit. Please arrange it.'

'Tomorrow, Ma!' said Shubhojit. 'You can go home. I can manage on my own.'

Kamladevi looked at Shubhojit helplessly but the irony of it was not lost on either of them.

32

The next day, Shubhojit was back in his office. There was nothing to keep him back at home; the family had gone their own separate ways and he was alone. He was like a log of wood drifting in the sea of humanity, all by himself; but he had memories to hold on to: good, bad and saucy: the kind of stuff life was made up of. And yet, he was tired and tired of it all.

'Am I happy,' thought Shubhojit, 'to be back in my office, in the familiar environment full of stacks of files awaiting my attention? Back to the routine of administrative rigmarole and tricky, knotty situations? To back-breaking, mind-numbing rounds of meetings, consultations and public hearings? Endless requests and pressures for recommendations regarding selections and appointments? The unending flow of DO (demi-official) letters and the long agendas being sent around at the last minute. To listen to the din of political clatter; the mischievous gossip of the secretarial staff; the noise of the waiting people; the constant going up and down of the lifts and the opening of their doors; the incessant ringing of the telephone bell. The constant ordering of tea, coffee, besan ki barfi and imarti for important visitors. And, above all, the strain of making a sincere effort to rise to every occasion and to the expectations of all the people involved. And the last but not the least, the nerve-racking ordeal of having plain-clothes CID men keep a constant vigil on one's activities if one happens to be on uneasy terms with the authorities.'

Shubhojit was dismayed at entertaining mean thoughts about the office on this first day after a long break.

'Don't I have anything better to think,' he wondered, 'since my office has always been almost an extension of myself? I have thrived on initiating innovative approaches to mind-boggling problems; I have woken up to the multiplicity of its complexities; I have scrupulously observed its rules and regulations; I have dreamt of my pet projects being completed in record time; in short, I have breathed and inhaled the very essence of public good, giving it the shape of a vision to be realized and a mission to be fulfilled. Why, then, do I now feel so disoriented and disheartened? Has the sudden realization of the futility and transience of life affected my drive for work and thwarted my capacity for clear thinking?'

Shubhojit was unable to drive away disturbing thoughts. His mind was in turmoil. There was a knock on the door and it opened slightly. Shubhojit responded with a 'Come in,' and his staff members entered and waited respectfully for his attention. He looked at them and smiled.

'Sir, how are you now?' asked the most senior among them. 'It is such a good feeling to have you back. Our office has been almost like an orphanage in your absence.'

'Oh! I am fine now,' answered Shubhojit, 'perfectly fine! Thank you.'

'Nevertheless, you must not exert yourself too much, Sir,' ventured another. 'Please take it a little easy.'

Shubhojit was touched by their concern and their loyalty to him. Their willingness to work with him! They had always put up with his long hours, his speed of working, as also with his idiosyncrasies. They had never objected to his calling them to work almost every Saturday and even on Sundays, if the situation demanded. They had been an excellent support system for him even at the cost of their own comfort or convenience.

He smiled and thanked them all for their support. He asked them for a cup of tea, a gentle indication to them to go back to their seats and take up work.

'What is the agenda for me today, Vishal?' Shubhojit asked his personal assistant.

'Nothing much, Sir!' said Vishal. 'There is no backlog; the officer-in-charge during your absence took care of the immediate matters. You can relax for a few days, Sir.'

Shubhojit said, 'I think I shall call on a few senior officers today. It is ages since I have had a cup of tea with them.'

Shubhojit took the day as it came: slow-paced, relaxed and without any sense of urgency. He called on the chief secretary (CS), the head of the civil service, who was deeply concerned about his health and asked him to take it slow and easy. 'Our work will continue the way it always has,' he told Shubhojit. 'We can take it only if we are fit, physically and mentally. And for that, we need to take care.'

Shubhojit responded warmly to his fatherly attitude and appreciated his concern. On his way out, he walked around casually in the corridors with which he was so familiar. He was happy to be there and back at work, but still, curiously, there lurked within him a peculiar restlessness.

'Do I want to go through it again, now that I have an option? How can I be sure?' he wondered. 'Is it time for me to give it all up? Is there anything new that I would like to take up which might make a difference to the system that has outlived my kind?'

Shubhojit remembered the time when he had first come to the secretariat. A young man then, he was full of energy, enthusiasm and enterprise. The gigantic building had overawed him; fascinated him with its capacity to house various organs of the administration, and with its work culture. It was, certainly, no ordinary building; it could put to shame the most outrageous of men; it could tame the wildest of them all; it could reward the most daring of men; it could harbour the most innovative of minds with its flexibility of interpretations; in short, it could do wonders! It was a great leveller—of human minds, instincts and intellect.

Many officers had come to this building; played their part and gone away, but it still stood tall and straight, a towering symbol of what the human mind, effort and industry could achieve; a beacon of inspiration in the most turbulent of times, turmoil or transition.

Shubhojit stood still, lost in thought: these corridors of power had defined his whole life; spanned his entire career and shaped his outlook. They had given him direction and drive; the motivation to move forward; to think ahead and out of the box; to dream and plan and leave, for the coming generations, a vision as legacy. This had been his altar of worship, where he had offered up his entire life and given thanks to God for every minute of it.

The corridors personified an entire system; a system that encapsulated in itself a whole lot of complexities and controversies, with a hint of complacency of sorts. A system that was capable of maintaining the status quo as well as generating an atmosphere conducive to change. Its complexity could not be breached; its controversies were beyond control, and its complacency beyond repair. The system was the creator as well as the destroyer, and its two aspects were complementary to each other. These corridors of power had fulfilled the secret wishes of ambitious men, and titillated public imagination with their unlimited powers.

Shubhojit stood dazed: he was unable to decide or come to terms with the realization that his continued presence here might be short-lived.

'Hi, Shubhojit!' There was a loud, surprised, exclamation. 'How are you? When did you resume work? You are looking well rested. Time for you to come back, my dear man. We have sorely missed you in the office.'

Shubhojit turned and saw Rajesh, his batchmate, smiling at him and trying to hug him. He responded as warmly, 'I am perfectly fine. I feel quite nostalgic being back. I was just thinking how time has flown. It seems as if it was only yesterday that all of us joined the service. And here we are, almost at the fag end of our career.'

'Oh, come on!' said Rajesh. 'Don't be so pessimistic, Shubhojit. Every day is a new day for us. There is always a challenge at every step, every minute. By now, we have become adept at handling anything and everything that comes our way.'

'Let's peep into a few rooms,' laughed Shubhojit, 'and see if anyone is free and can offer us a cup of tea!'

'Along with besan ki barfi!' Rajesh smiled gleefully.

'You are still young at heart, Rajesh! How do you manage it?'

'If we don't smile or laugh or joke in our rare moments of leisure, Shubhojit, we shall all go mad. The procedural mayhem won't let us breathe. We have got to make every effort to keep sane,' said Rajesh.

They passed by the room of another batchmate and decided to look in. Sriniwas was sitting in his chair, engrossed in looking through a stack of files. It was a couple of moments before he noticed Rajesh and Shubhojit standing before him.

'How come you are so busy?' asked Rajesh.

'Shubhojit! It is lovely to have you back once again,' said Sriniwas. 'I suppose we can rest only when health demands it. What an irony! I have often wondered at it.'

'Yes, of course! The system does not know the word *saturation point*. We are looked upon as robots, devoid of all feelings, expected to deliver results or reach targets at the drop of a hat, and without any goof-ups. There is never any room for *ifs* and *buts* or even alternatives. It might leave you totally drained of energy—physical, mental and emotional—but the system has never made it its business.'

'And to add to that,' said Rajesh, 'you are considered worthy of accolades only if you drop dead or collapse while on duty!'

'Well!' said Sriniwas, 'let's be fair to our seniors too. They themselves are in the same boat. Rest or relaxation—contrary to public perception—is a rare luxury in the service. A troubled psyche might be hidden behind the calmest face, behind that carefully maintained front against scrutiny by the public or by the juniors and subordinates.'

'Very well said, Sriniwas!' said Shubhojit. 'It takes a heavy toll on their health as well as personal lives. The only option, as well as remedy, for them is endurance.'

'And that too without a syllable of protest or even a casual utterance of a feeling of discontent,' said Rajesh, 'coupled with a readiness to face the brickbats or the blame game.'

'What can be most damaging to one's mind and emotional health is the effort of repressing one's feelings,' Sriniwas concluded.

The buzzer sounded and he picked up the phone and

exclaimed loudly, 'Oh, please do come and join us, Narender! We are all here together, chatting and waiting for a cup of tea, samosas and besan ki barfi to be served. Come quickly.'

Sriniwas hung up, called the peon and gave the order.

'Narender is joining us. Let me call a few others too, if they are free and available. Let's celebrate Shubhojit's return. It will be like old times.'

Manreet, Nagpal, Rajrup, Pawan and Harbans joined them. The atmosphere was once again charged with laughter, informality and a sense of relaxation. They reminisced about the old times; the old enthusiasm and the sense of idealism that had marked their persona in the initial years. They had lived the moments—though hurried—to the nth degree and with grace that had come naturally to them at that time.

They talked about their successors, the following generation, and wondered whether the same thing could be said about them. Their generation had tried to uphold the values and etiquette that their predecessors taught them; at the same time, they had sought to match the quick pace and the changing sensibilities of the new entrants in the field. They had tried to provide a stable bridge between the two, tried their level best not to hurt the sentiments of either. The effort and the compromises they had had to make had been entirely their own choice or decision. As long as they were fine with it, extraneous things had not mattered. It had all been a part of the package.

The door opened and the peon walked in with cups of tea and snacks. They looked at one another, winked and laughed heartily!

33

Shubhojit regained his spirits a little during the spontaneous get-together with his batchmates. He spent the rest of the day in looking through papers and re-familiarizing himself with the surroundings. He tried to put all disturbing thoughts out of his mind and get into the normal routine. Somehow, it wasn't the same for him, as it had always been. Somehow, a crack had opened up between the real world and the world of his thoughts and sensibilities. The more he tried to mend it, the harder it became, and the effort left him exhausted.

The approaching evening brought back thoughts of home and family. He quaked at the thought of going home. Once again, it was no longer a home; it had gone back into being a house: empty of love; empty spaces; food which no longer tasted good. Gone was the cheeriness, the optimism, the informal communication and the reminiscing. Shubhojit was in no hurry to get back. He whiled away his time, attending to trivial issues till he could no longer avoid the inevitable.

On his way home, he decided to peep into the officers' club. It was a long time since he had last been there and he missed the friendly interaction with his colleagues from other cadres and services.

'Hi, Shubhojit!' came an anxious voice. 'Good to see you back. Hope you are fine now.'

Harbhajan, another of Shubhojit's batchmates, was tapping on his shoulder and looking at him affectionately.

'Harbhajan,' smiled Shubhojit. 'I am alive and kicking. What's going on here?'

'Nothing, yaar,' said Harbhajan, 'the same old routine. We work till late in the office every day, and meet our friends here for a cup of coffee or a glass of wine. It is a good diversion and some relief from the work.'

A few more officers gathered around Shubhojit, all visibly happy to see him back among them.

'Hey, Shubhojit!' joked Ranjit. 'You should come here every day and have a glass of red wine. It is supposed to be good for the heart.'

'I think that's exactly what I should be doing,' agreed Shubhojit. 'But, I am happy to be here today and I thank you all for your concern.'

They talked about ordinary matters: families, friends, just simple delightful things that add meaning to life. None was interested in discussing things that happened in the office; their minds needed a rest from the drudgery, and their body language expressed it. The unpredictability of life—as exemplified by Shubhojit's unexpected illness—had taught them to live in the moment and deal with the future when it knocked at their door. Who knew? Who had seen the future? They had cups of coffee and tea, talked and laughed, and finally decided to disperse.

Shubhojit came back to an empty house and felt troubled by its emptiness. There was only Bahadur to welcome him or give him company. The house seemed so depressing in the absence of his family; he sorely missed his mother's patronizing talks and his children's energizing, pleasant company. Now, even Yashodhra would find it hard to visit him lacking the pretext of meeting Neelakshi and Hemant. The temporary semblance of a family life had vanished.

Shubhojit had an early dinner and retired to his bedroom in a rather sombre mood. Melancholy thoughts again raised their ugly head in his mind, and he tried to shake them off. Different memories haunted him, flowed over him like a flood, and he reeled under their impact. He mulled over his experiences: with the authorities; politicians; colleagues; subordinates; during normal times and while dealing with disaster situations. Shubhojit felt a volcano erupting in his chest and a great disquiet creeping through his consciousness.

His career graph had been like a tapestry; a weaving of knots and colours into a plausible pattern and an attempt to make it an integral part of a bigger pattern or system. He remembered his struggle with the system; its votaries; the parasites who constantly clawed their way towards its core, leaving it hollow and crippled; its so-called benefactors who used it to advance their own interests.

His professional life had been a constant struggle against odds; against differing ideologies; against sagging value systems and falling standards of norms, chivalry and etiquette. He had tried to put up a brave fight, tried to hold on to his own ideals, and he had suffered in the process but he was always determined never to give up. He was not the only one to suffer; his suffering had percolated down to his family as well. Yashodhra, like him, was left disoriented many times; in every way, she had had to adjust much more than he had. Both had tried their best to protect their children from the fall-outs of these problems till they were grown up enough to understand them and deal with them on their own. It occurred to him—not for the first time—that they had not been entirely successful.

And now, he was feeling disconnected: from the official

world; his colleagues; his friends; in fact, with the whole of mankind, including his family, to some extent. His ties, emotional or otherwise, lay severed for the time being. For some time, at least, he wanted to get free; of everything and everybody; he wanted to be alone and not worry too much about instincts or emotions like love, affection, compassion, hatred, greed, fear or pity.

Had his idealism driven him to this saturation point, he wondered. Was he completely burnt out? He had done enough to serve people, to do his little bit as best as he could and, now, he no longer wanted to be responsible for their welfare. They could take care of themselves, and perhaps in a much better way, he was sure of that. He wanted to take a break and seriously explore the true significance of words like courage, glory, honour, commitment, idealism etc. Would it be possible for him to disengage himself from the doings of humanity?

He wanted to be alone in the company of Nature and live, or try to live, as ancient man had, in direct communion with creation. He had developed a serious urge to lead a simple life for a while—a life that catered only to man's basic needs; a life away from the prying eyes of society; away from consideration of public approval or censure. He wanted to give up the instinct to excel; he no longer wanted to be judged by others and be judgemental himself. He wanted to redefine the word *ambition* and to widen the definition of success. He did not want to carry the burden or baggage of official pressures, or societal norms and compulsions, or follow a stereotyped routine of any kind. He just wanted to be himself, if that was possible.

'Is it a tall order?' he lay on his bed, wondering. 'Is it possible? Can I turn my back on the world and its activities for a year or two? Until I feel thoroughly refreshed, with my priorities clearly drawn in my mind? Until I am face to face with my own self? Until my faith in mankind is restored through a fruitful communion with Nature? Until I regain childlike simplicity and innocence, if possible.'

Shubhojit was wandering in a maze of troublesome thoughts that showed no signs of abating. His mind was reeling with unnerving mental images; his emotions were muddled, and his body was numb with fatigue. He wanted to sleep but sleep eluded him and, overcome by a torrent of memories, he continued thinking.

'The journey of life is a progression from innocence to corruption, from primal instincts to sophisticated artifice, from instinctual wisdom to acquired education based on concocted theories, lop-sided interpretation and formulated philosophies.'

'Life is a vicious circle,' he thought. 'First, we are in a hurry to sever ourselves from our roots, break all connections with tradition in our march towards modernity, to immerse ourselves in worldly pleasures till we can take it no more, or till we reach a peak and then...then starts the downward slide... towards the process of simplification of activities...trying to get rid of the useless paraphernalia surrounding us, learning to terminate false relationships, turning towards things that will take us back to our roots. There comes a point in the life of a man when he wants to shed everything: inhibitions, pressures, false emotions, modern gadgets, printed word, expression of innermost feelings etc, till he is left in his true naked form, mentally and emotionally, so that he can take a step towards spiritualism and ultimate communion with God.'

Shubhojit trembled at the idea. 'Have I reached that stage?'

He reasoned in his mind, 'Perhaps, yes! What else is left in the world for me to achieve? Professionally, I have reached the pinnacle. Yashodhra, though still unsure and doubtful about the appropriateness of her decision, took a call for which I had no right to begrudge her. Hemant and Neelakshi are all set on their professional path and will gradually climb the ladder of success, with or without my help. I have reached a stage in life from where I can look back, if not with full satisfaction, also not with dissatisfaction. Life has been good to me; sweet and sour; with varying degrees of success on different fronts, and also filled with moments tinged with remorse and helplessness.'

Shubhojit wanted to leave all this behind him for some time. He wanted to look ahead; stare open-eyed into the future; march backwards; reach the point from where he had started life with stars in his eyes, energy in his blood and enthusiasm in his heart. At the same time, he wanted to go back to his roots; he *needed* to go back in order to attain a mental equilibrium; to achieve that level of stoicism that his mother had reached by dint of rustic common sense, intelligence and a calm acceptance of fate, and who was still leading a full life.

'Should I take leave from office for some time?' Shubhojit toyed with the idea that had been simmering in his mind for some time. 'Maybe for a year or two, depending on how I react to a sojourn in the lap of nature, away from the back-breaking, mind-numbing routine of office, but not too far away from humanity.'

Sifting his rampant ideas carefully and reasoning clearly in the privacy of his thoughts, Shubhojit almost made up his mind and reached a conclusion.

'Yes,' he thought, 'the time is ripe, ripe for me to take a decision, a decision that is likely to raise many eyebrows; a decision that may disturb or please many and also make many smile uncomfortably; a decision that will not go down well with the authorities, that might lead them to sit back, ponder and deconstruct its attitudinal nuances, as also the reason for the discontent. It will ruffle many feathers in the corridors of power, lead to heated discussions and make people wonder about the urgency of such a decision.'

He let out a deep breath. 'Will anyone understand my reasons for taking such a call?' he wondered. 'Do I care? Probably not! No, not at all!'

His streak of stubborn independence had taken the better of him. His mind made up, he quickly fell asleep.

He slept well and got up a little late. He felt light in his mind; the way one feels when a great load is off one's shoulders. It was the beginning of a new day outside, with nature in its full glory: the clear sky radiant with the rays of the morning sun; the twittering sound of early-morning birds and the subtle fragrance of the dew-laden flowers. Shubhojit's heart was brimming with joy. He was ready to face another day, rather, an unusual day.

Once in the secretariat, he headed straight for the CS's office. He expected him to be there as he usually came in before many of them arrived. His personal secretary informed him that he was not yet in. Shubhojit asked for an urgent appointment with the boss.

'Very well, Sir! I shall let you know immediately.'

'I shall be in my office, waiting for the call!' said Shubhojit.

34

$\mathcal{S}$HUBHOJIT SAT in his office chair, feeling a bit uncomfortable. His heart was beating fast. The enormity of his surprising decision had ruffled the calmness of his mind. The absence of the CS increased his sense of uncertainty because he wanted his dilemma to be over as soon as possible. He had made up his mind and there was no going back now. He needed a respite; he needed it greatly and he was looking forward to it.

His personal staff was rather surprised that he had come in so early. They thought he could take things a little easy for now. The office was usually a matter of routine and offered nothing new with its mechanical mindset and stereotyped mode of functioning. There was a knock on the door and his personal assistant entered the room with a stack of files.

'Sir,' he said, 'these need your immediate attention.'

'Leave them on the table,' said Shubhojit, 'I shall take a look.'

The PA did as directed and went out. Shubhojit tried to gather his thoughts and decided to have a look at the files. He picked up one and opened it. Just then, the buzzer sounded:

'Sir,' said his PA, 'there is a call from the CS's office.'

'Yes!' said Shubhojit. 'Please connect.'

'Sir,' said the voice at the other end, 'the CS is in the office and can meet you immediately.'

'I'll be there right away,' said Shubhojit and hung up. He left a message with his staff and walked towards the CS's office.

Once there, it was only a couple of moments before he was sitting face to face with the CS.

'How are you, Shubhojit?' smiled the CS. 'I hope all is well. So, tell me what brings you to me, so early in the morning?'

'Sir,' said Shubhojit, 'I have something very important to discuss with you. And for that, I need your full attention for a while. It depends entirely on your convenience and I can come some other time if you are not free right now.'

'Oh, no, Shubhojit,' said the CS, 'There is no government business which cannot wait for half an hour and that too, first thing in the morning. Feel absolutely free to talk. I am all attention.'

'Sir,' Shubhojit hesitated, 'I was just thinking...'

'Thinking what, Shubhojit?' the CS was a little alarmed. He picked up the phone and left a message that he was not to be disturbed for some time.

'I was just thinking, Sir,' said Shubhojit, 'that I have had enough.'

'Enough of what?'

'Enough of my stint with the administration, Sir!' The words poured out of Shubhojit in a rush whose intensity he was unable to control. 'Enough of my job; enough of my robotic life; enough of having to make forced decisions; enough of having to stifle the voice of conscience at times; enough of ignoring the thin line of demarcation between the personal and the professional; enough of sacrificing my personal life and concerns in the larger interest...'

'Slow down, Shubhojit!' the CS cut him short with a bewildered look. 'What are you talking about? What has suddenly come over you? You are one of our finest officers. The entire service is proud of you and your achievements. We can't let you feel low like this. We shall do all that we can to perk up your spirits.'

'That's precisely the point, Sir,' answered Shubhojit. 'I want to get out of the system of controls and allowances. I want to break free of the shackles of rules and regulations. I want to feel free, breathe free, eat free and sleep free. I don't know whether this is possible or whether it is just one of my quirks. I want to be closer to mother earth and re-experience nature in its purest form. At least for the time being...' Shubhojit was clearly overwhelmed.

The CS was taken aback by the torrent of passion from Shubhojit, who was usually restrained in demeanour and speech. He took a long and steady look at Shubhojit, trying to ascertain his state of mind and also decide how to best deal with this situation.

'Shubhojit,' he said in a sombre tone, 'I understand you need a break from our kind of drudgery. Your period of convalescence has given you time to ponder on these matters. Now that you are well and have regained your health, you need a change of place.'

'That's exactly what I want, Sir,' interrupted Shubhojit, 'a change of place, circumstances and maybe even means of keeping myself busy.'

'I see your point,' said the CS. 'Take another fifteen days off or even a month, go to a hill station or a health resort, preferably with a friend or a family member and relax. Just relax. I can assure you that no one will disturb you or even ask for your whereabouts. That's my promise to you.'

Shubhojit was silent for a long time. Perhaps he was trying to gather his thoughts or to measure his words, or perhaps both. He was at a loss how to articulate his real intentions without being the least bit offensive to such a caring head of the fraternity.

'Sir, I meant the same thing but perhaps in a different way...' Shubhojit's voice trailed off.

'What are you trying to say, Shubhojit?' The CS was puzzled. 'Come out clean with whatever you have in your heart.'

'Sir,' said Shubhojit with a gulp, 'I am at a stage where I can afford to look back as well as forward. I look back at my career with a sense of satisfaction. I have no regrets. I have always tried to do my best and do what I thought was right. I have been praised as well as censured, and was indifferent to both. I have enjoyed the support of my seniors, who helped me realize my pet projects, even though they looked difficult at that time. I couldn't have done better and that makes me a happy man today.'

'Then, where lies the problem, Shubhojit?'

'Sir,' said Shubhojit with a grim look, 'I feel I have lost out on many accounts. We bureaucrats are so entrenched in our safe and secure ivory tower that we lose touch with our own selves. We become oblivious to our surroundings, neighbourhood, environment, family, society, as well as our inner reality.'

'Shubhojit, now you are testing my patience. Say what you have to say!' There was a tone of impatience in the CS's voice.

'Sir, I want to call it *quits*!' Shubhojit blurted out.

'What?' The CS looked at him with disbelief.

'I have had enough, Sir!' said Shubhojit, 'I want to opt for VRS—Voluntary Retirement Scheme—and be done with it.'

'I hope you are in your right senses, Shubhojit, and have given enough thought to your ideas. Don't be impulsive and take a hasty decision.'

'I have carefully weighed my options, Sir!' said Shubhojit. 'Such decisions are not taken overnight. I have been toying with this idea for a long time and my decision is the result of a lot of thinking.'

'Have you taken a final decision, Shubhojit? Have you consulted your family?'

'Family?' smiled Shubhojit. 'That is just a concept for me, Sir!'

'Come on, Shubhojit! You have your children's future to take care of.'

'Sir, they are too young to understand my reasons for taking such a decision,' said Shubhojit, 'and it certainly won't affect Yashodhra in any way. My mother has always supported me in whatever I have done in my life. Nobody else has a right to question my decision or is likely to suffer from the after-effects of such a step.'

'What are your plans for the future, Shubhojit? What do you intend to do? Have you thought about the repercussions of such a decision and its impact on your future?'

'Yes, Sir, I have,' said Shubhojit. 'I wish to lead a simple life with bare necessities, devoid of all luxuries and pretensions. I wish to see whether it is possible for a man to survive in natural surroundings, away from the humdrum of city life. I wish to make a decent living and yet be close to earth and the common people. And for how long? I don't know, but it is worth giving it a try.'

'New concepts and ideas appear fascinating, Shubhojit,' said the CS, 'till they are tried out. You may be in for a surprise too. After all, man is a social animal and he is happiest living among his own kind. One can't run away from people or denigrate them for what are natural human instincts.'

'I don't plan to run away from society or the world as such, Sir,' said Shubhojit. 'I only want to lead a simple life among simple people and in simple surroundings.'

'Everything is simple, Shubhojit,' said the CS. 'It is the people who make it complex by adding different variants. But I see sense in what you are saying. You *do* need a change of environment. But you don't have to put in your papers for that. All you need is a reasonably long break from established norms and routine. Try it out and only then take a final call.'

'Sir, I am left with a little less than four years of service. I might as well avail the VRS.'

'That's quite some time, Shubhojit,' said the CS. 'I suggest that you take a long break first, see how you respond to your new, changed scenario, and then make a final decision. That way, you will save yourself the regret of quitting the service in case you should review your decision. Better play safe!'

Shubhojit smiled. 'Yes, we are experts in that, Sir!'

'Think it over, Shubhojit!'

'How long a leave is it possible for you to sanction me, Sir?'

'How long do you want?'

'Initially, at least for a year! Would it be possible?'

'Certainly,' said the CS, 'and that's my promise to you. I shall see to it that nothing goes amiss. Think the whole thing over with a cool mind, write your application and send it across to me at the earliest.'

'Sir,' asked Shubhojit looking straight into his eyes, 'do you approve of my decision? Do you, in your personal capacity, see the relevance of me taking such a decision?'

The CS looked at him straight, smiled and said, 'I wish I could join you too, Shubhojit. I wish I had the guts to take such a decision. But I am not so lucky, after all.'

'I shall always be indebted to you, Sir!'

'Tell me about your plans! Where would you like to go? Where would you stay? What would you do? How would you keep yourself busy? Would you be far from human habitation?'

'No, Sir!' said Shubhojit. 'I wouldn't be very far from people. In fact, mine would be a retreat only from this artificial life that blunts all sensibilities—physical, emotional and spiritual. I want to live near my village, where I can belong to the soil; where I can enjoy the fresh mornings; where I can watch the rising sun; where I can listen to the twittering sounds of early birds; where I can see the dew-fresh beauty of the morning flowers; where I can plant a few saplings and watch them grow; where I can have a kitchen garden and tend to my own fruit trees; where I can keep a cow and a buffalo and milk them in the morning; where I can keep pace with my dogs when I go for a walk in the nearby bani woods; where anybody and everybody can walk into my small hut at any hour of the day and enjoy a simple, frugal meal; where formality would not be an issue and pretence not a weapon; where to exist would be to live and to live would be to enjoy, and enjoyment would lead to a communion with the creator and His creation.'

The CS, mesmerized, was unable to hold back his tears. He got up, embraced Shubhojit and said, 'Go, my friend, follow your instincts! I would love to join you any time. The right time will come for me too, I am sure. And yes, send your application tomorrow. Don't delay.'

35

Shubhojit returned home in the evening, determined and satisfied with the decision he had made. The heart-to-heart talk with the CS had acted as a catharsis for him. He felt unburdened and happy as a lark. He didn't need much time to wind things up. The members of his family were all set on their paths, and he didn't owe any explanation to them. Bahadur could continue to look after the house as long as he was in a position to keep it up and then, later, he would take the next step. He had set the ball rolling, and now, he wanted to leave, and leave quickly. It was time to inform Bahadur about the future course of things and make him understand. Shubhojit sent for him.

'Bahadur,' he said in an affectionate tone, 'you have to take care of the house in my absence.'

'Absence, Sahib?' Bahadur was confused.

'I am going away, Bahadur. I am going away for a long time.'

'Going where, Sir?' asked Bahadur, almost in tears. 'You haven't even fully recovered.'

'Oh, I am perfectly fine, Bahadur,' said Shubhojit. 'Don't worry about me. You have been a big help to me. You have always been a member of my family.'

'But where are you going, Sahib?'

'Bahadur, I hope you will understand!' said Shubhojit. 'I want to go away from this city and my work. I want to get out of this mechanical routine for some time, at least. I want to feel free as a bird. I only want to eat, drink, sleep and do my own work. I want to interact with people without any agenda or angle. I want to detoxify my soul. I am going back to a place near my village, where I shall be away from this busy, empty world and yet be an integral part of life.'

'Sahib, let me come with you and help,' pleaded Bahadur. 'I assure you I shall not bother you in the least bit.'

'Let me go alone initially, Bahadur,' said Shubhojit, 'while you take care of things here. I promise that I shall send for you if I decide to live there permanently. That's a promise.' Shubhojit patted his back.

'Shall I serve dinner, Sahib?'

'Ah, yes, Bahadur! I am very hungry.'

Shubhojit had a good meal and enjoyed every bit of it. He was very fond of Bahadur who had been with him through thick and thin, and had always understood the constraints of his job better than anybody else in the family. And he had expected nothing in return.

'Many a time, an understanding of one's limitations comes from a quarter from where you least expect it.' Shubhojit wondered and smiled at the irony.

He had the night all to himself: long, dark, peaceful and lovely. Time and space, both at his command for the time being. He sat on the recliner in his study and lazed into indifference. He thought about his past few years in the service that already seemed so remote and almost unreal. They seemed to have gone now and might soon be obliterated from his memory too.

'And then, there would remain nothing,' wondered Shubhojit. 'A big chunk of one's life frittered away in useless pursuits, till there remained nothing except the lone man himself, naked to the soul and bereft of all emotions, instincts and sensations; an outer shell of his former self, capable only of tottering towards eternity.'

Shubhojit fell asleep. Though his body rested, his mind seemed to be in a trance where time stood still. He tried to fumble his way out, floating weightlessly. Suddenly, the air cleared all around him and he saw a light above, beckoning him with its purity and radiance. His mind seemed to be getting newly enlightened and he found himself filled with a strange feeling of contentment. He could clearly see his way ahead. All doubts were cleared from his mind and the fear of uncertainty vanished into thin air. A sudden jolt and Shubhojit woke up. It took him a moment to realize that he had been dreaming of things remote, far-flung from this world. He got up, went to his room and slept till late in the morning.

The sun was shining bright when he opened the window of his room. He looked at the deep blue sky and inhaled the fresh air. It was a new day—clear, bright, soft and pleasant. He was going to make a fresh start in his life, in a way that he had only dreamt of till now. The moment had arrived to turn it into a reality and get rid of all doubts in his mind.

'Shall I be successful?' There still lurked a doubt in his mind. 'Shall I be able to break free of the past in totality? Shall I be able to bring my soul into communion with the ultimate truth? This is going to be another challenge! Or perhaps, pleasure? Only time will tell! But I am looking forward to it with all my heart and soul.'

Shubhojit got ready in a jiffy. He had a lot of various formalities to take care of. He had to complete half-finished tasks on many fronts. His leave would take a few days to get sanctioned and, meanwhile, he could utilize the time to take care of things.

He wanted to inform Yashodhra. Maybe she would understand now; maybe she would not. Did it matter to him? He was not sure. What about Hemant and Neelakshi? He was not sure of their reactions either. They were perhaps too young to understand the reasons behind such a decision. They would understand by and by, as they grew older, thought Shubhojit. He was quite sure of Kamladevi, his mother. She would not only understand it but also welcome it. She would appreciate the logic behind it as well as the emotional, spiritual compulsions that drove him. Perhaps she had known all along that Shubhojit would eventually take such a decision. She was the only one who knew what was going on in his mind. He would take it up with his immediate family first, thought Shubhojit. He dialled Yashodhra's number.

'Hello! How are you, Shubhojit? Hope all is well!' answered Yashodhra.

'Yes, all is fine, thank you!' said Shubhojit. 'Yashodhra, I want to share something with you. I have decided to take a sabbatical. I am going to live near our village for about a year. I just need to de-stress. I thought I would like to tell you.'

'Oh!' Yashodhra's surprise was evident. 'Isn't that a sudden decision?'

'Not really. For some time, I have been debating about the advisability as well as the repercussions of my decision,' said Shubhojit. 'It is only now that I no longer have any doubt about it. I hope you understand.'

'Yes, Shubhojit, I understand your reasons perfectly well, and I whole-heartedly support you. I am sure it will do you good.'

'Do you mean it, Yashodhra?'

'Certainly, you can be sure, Shubhojit. Tell me, if ever I

should want to come over for a short stay, would you have any objection to it?'

'Don't be silly, Yashodhra!' Shubhojit was clearly overwhelmed. 'My house, wherever, will always be open to you. Only you and our children have the privilege of not ever asking me before coming. Do you understand?'

'Yes, I do, Shubhojit!' said Yashodhra, trying to keep her emotions in check. 'And I wish you all the best in this new phase of your life. I am sure it will bring a lot of peace in your life.'

'Thank you, Yashodhra! Bye, sweetheart!'

Yashodhra hung up.

Shubhojit felt it was the right time to talk to his children too. He rang up Hemant first.

'Hi, Papa! How are you?' asked Hemant.

'Let me not mince words with you, Hemant,' said Shubhojit 'I want to tell you that I have decided to go on a long leave for about a year. And I am looking forward to leading an almost primitive life to answer some of the questions that have been troubling me for a long time.'

'Would you like to share those with me, Papa?' Hemant's tone was serious.

'In time to come, yes, Hemant!' answered Shubhojit. 'I would certainly like my son to understand the reasons behind all my decisions. Right now, maybe you should concentrate on your studies. We'll talk about it in detail when we meet next.'

'How soon would that be, Papa?'

'Don't worry about it, son. You can come to me or talk to me whenever you feel like. Your mother, too, is always there for you. Remember that.'

'Yes, Papa!' Hemant couldn't correlate his words and thoughts.

'Bye, son! Take care!' And Shubhojit hung up.

Shubhojit felt much lighter. The worst was over for him. He only needed to talk to Neelakshi now. He was sure Yashodhra had told her by now. His phone rang just then and he saw that it was a call from Neelakshi. Shubhojit smiled and picked up the receiver.

'Hi, Papa! What's wrong with you? Mom told me you are taking a long break and going away,' Neelakshi was clearly agitated. 'What has come over you suddenly, Papa?'

'Take it easy, my dear,' Shubhojit tried to comfort her. 'Haven't I come a long way in life? Don't I need some relaxation?'

'This is no way, Papa!' insisted Neelakshi. 'We could all have taken a holiday together and you could have relaxed. Where was the necessity to resort to such an extreme measure?'

Shubhojit laughed aloud. He appreciated Neelakshi's way of registering her displeasure. She had always had a way with words and used them to great effect. He liked the fact that his children continued to be so concerned about him. He once again felt loved, and that was a comforting thought.

'Papa, will you say something?' urged Neelakshi. 'I am talking to you.'

Shubhojit laughed again. 'Yes, Neelakshi, I am listening to you. And don't be so angry with me, dear. I can assure you that this retreat of mine is going to be a short one and I shall be back among all of you within a year or so. Let's stay away from each other for a while. I am sure our reunion will compensate for our temporary separation.'

'Papa, must you always have your way?'

'Has it really been so, my dear?' Shubhojit smiled. 'I think I have only listened to you most times.'

'When are you planning to leave, Papa?' asked Neelakshi in a dejected tone.

'As soon as my leave comes through! Shouldn't be very long, though, Neelakshi! I can tie up the loose ends meanwhile.'

'Good luck, Papa!' said Neelakshi. 'I am sure you know well what you are doing. Can I come and see you whenever I want?'

'Since when has my daughter needed my permission to meet me?'

'Hope to see you soon, Papa!' said Neelakshi. 'Perhaps you know I am as incorrigible as you. Aren't I?'

'Yes, my dear! God bless you!'

Shubhojit was back to his own self. He had a long day ahead. His mind was light and his mood cheerful. He was filled with positive energy at the thought of pursuing his dream as faithfully as he had lived his professional life. He got ready and set out for his office.

The sky above was clear and the sun was strong. The air was fresh and invigorating, and it had a curious clarity. The surrounding bushes were in bloom. The silent wind carried the scent along with it, and the rays of the sun spread a golden glow over everything that was visible to the eye. Shubhojit looked around. It was spring for him, literally and symbolically.

36

Shubhojit arrived at his isolated abode on the outskirts of the village at the weekend. He was quite tickled by the idea of a 'weekend.' Would it mean the same as before? Would weekdays matter as much as they had earlier? The frantic race to meet with deadlines on specific days used to be alleviated by the thought of a couple of days of leisure and relaxation. Human beings, especially those who were involved in a mad race of one kind or another, really did need the relief of a solitary sojourn at the foothills of mountains or in a vast wilderness, where mother earth ruled and sustained their needs, and the birds did most of the talking.

Shubhojit knew instantly that he had made the right choice. He had not followed his dream exactly as he had envisioned it but had made a few changes in the larger interest and taking into account his delicate health. Though fit now, he still needed to be cautious and not undertake any heavy physical activity. He had made arrangements for his small hut-like habitation to be neat, clean and comfortable. It had reasonable modern amenities but enough scope for a person to do without them.

His arrival in the village was marked with a kind of euphoria. The village people were curious to see him, meet with him and talk to him. His mother had been approached and prevailed upon to help them in this regard. She had been waiting for his arrival ever since she came to know of his decision. In fact, she had been a part of all the preparations there. Being a mother, she knew exactly what her son might want or need or dislike. She knew Shubhojit would want to be all by himself and avoid intrusion of any kind. She had promised the people that she would facilitate the initial meeting with him and, after that, village life would follow its usual course.

Shubhojit touched his mother's feet as she received him with a warm hug. 'Welcome to your roots, son,' said Kamladevi. 'The slow-paced simple life of the village and the fresh air will do you good, I am sure.'

'I too think so!' smiled Shubhojit. 'Hasn't life come full circle, Ma? I started my life from here, courted the outside world, but now have come back to it, seeking peace and solitude.'

'We are all very happy to see you!' was the unanimous greeting of the people who had gathered there to welcome him. 'It is our privilege that you will be spending so much time here. We hope you thoroughly enjoy your stay with us. Do let us know if you need anything.'

'Oh, thank you so much for everything,' smiled Shubhojit. 'I already feel at home.'

'Home is where the heart is!' laughed an elderly man. 'It is very difficult to ignore the call of the blood and the instincts. You have come of your own accord, listening to your inner voice and I am sure you will find what you are looking for.'

Shubhojit was touched that the simple village people had thought so much about his homecoming.

'Nobody is going to impinge on your privacy here, Shubhojit,' said another. 'You will be on your own for as long as you like. Nobody will bother you, but you are most welcome to come, visit, talk and interact with us whenever you feel like.'

'Oh, thank you, so much!' Shubhojit appreciated their sentiments and kind words. He liked their informality and lack of pretentiousness. They would leave him alone if that was what he wanted. They would be willing to give support of any kind if he let them. He felt he had finally arrived at a place where he could be himself without the fear of being judged or censured or ridiculed.

'Do people matter much to me now?' wondered Shubhojit. 'Have I sought solitude only to get away from all mankind?'

Kamladevi had been studying Shubhojit's face intently and could imagine his thoughts at this point. She decided he needed rest and wanted to be on his own.

'Let's keep our interaction for another day since he is going to be here for some time,' she said. 'Shubhojit, if you could keep your luggage in place, look around and check whether everything is all right, maybe then, everybody could go back, and we could meet another day.'

'Yes, Ma! Don't worry about anything! I am home, aren't I? Stay for a while and then I shall walk you back to the haveli.'

Taking their cue, the people folded their hands in a goodwill gesture and left. Though Shubhojit had enjoyed talking to them, he felt that he had somehow fallen apart as far as fellowship was concerned. It wouldn't have mattered much to him whether he talked to anybody or not. It wouldn't matter much to him whether they came back here to be with him or not. It would depend on how he responded to their efforts at intimacy.

'Shubhojit,' said Kamladevi, 'let's eat together so I too can leave.'

'Yes, Ma,' said Shubhojit, 'I am hungry.'

Mother and son sat down for the informal, simple, healthy

meal, in rustic surroundings. She had taken care to make food according to Shubhojit's liking: bajre ki roti with butter and jaggery, bathua raita, sarson ka saag and chutney. There was no need for anything else. This was what she used to prepare for Shubhojit, day after day, when he was a child and living with her. She knew he had always missed the food that she made for him. This would be her gesture of welcoming her son to the new world in which he wanted to live now.

She saw admiration and a deep sense of gratitude in Shubhojit's eyes. She knew that look very well and felt immensely happy. She would love to feed him again, as in the old days. Could life be the same again, she wondered! It certainly had come full circle!

The meal over, Shubhojit walked his mother to their ancestral home. The walk reminded him of his childhood days when he used to wander through the village, its narrow lanes and by-lanes, and then go home. He looked around as he held his mother's hand firmly. He wondered at how situations change for human beings while nature and the other natural elements remained the same. It was only a few decades ago that his mother held his hand and guided him along these village roads, preparing him to walk on the path of life. And now, a decade short of half a century, he was doing the same for his mother. He was happy to be with her once again.

They were nearing their destination. As they walked along, they were the object of curious and surprised glances from people they knew so well. Acknowledging their greetings with folded hands, Shubhojit and Kamladevi stopped occasionally to exchange a pleasantry or indulge in chitchat. Nothing was unfamiliar to Shubhojit, except the younger lot, as he dug back into his memory. He enjoyed what he was doing:

walking aimlessly; not having an agenda of any kind; meeting people randomly; eating whatever came his way or was offered affectionately; talking freely without bothering about being politically correct. He felt truly liberated.

Kamladevi, meanwhile, had also been undergoing similar emotions. Shubhojit had visited the village occasionally in the past but this was an altogether different situation. Her son had been a super achiever in his life and career. He had always been a role model for the youth of his village. His name had commanded respect from all. His coming back home to renew his natal bond and to discover his real self was a matter of pride not only for her but for his village as well. It might set a trend, she thought.

And now, she felt elated that her son was escorting her home. It filled her with a special joy. Her attention was caught by the twittering sound of a bird in a nearby bush. A female bird was trying to feed her young one which was fluttering around making all kinds of noises. Finally, she succeeded in putting the morsel of food into its tiny beak and calming it down. Kamladevi laughed aloud as she watched them nestle together.

The ancestral haveli stood right in front of them: a towering symbol of their family and of an era gone by. It again reminded Shubhojit of the eternal flux called time; time that waits for none; time, the mighty puppeteer that keeps human beings on their toes. Shubhojit remembered the sayings of the sages and scriptures that it was the sanctity of a place that beckoned an individual to find his moorings. The destinies of houses, places and individuals were somehow linked in a way that was incomprehensible to the human eye.

Kamladevi and Shubhojit entered the haveli to loud cheers

from their near and distant relatives. Shubhojit was back where he belonged, where he had always belonged. Kamladevi had known this truth, instinctively or otherwise, he could not tell. But it had taken him a lifetime to discover it and finally arrive at this inevitability.

The haveli entrance opened onto a big *aangan* that served as a common sitting room for all visitors. Fairly big and spacious, it had a number of cots which were used for casual, comfortable sitting. Shubhojit and Kamladevi made themselves at ease and drank hot milk that had been kept ready for their expected arrival.

Shubhojit rested, talked at length with his relatives, and laughed heartily while Kamladevi lay on the cot, eyes shut. Shubhojit was in no hurry to leave as he had a lot of time on his hands and no deadlines to meet. He could take his own time setting up his things in the hut and starting a new life.

It was close to a couple of hours before Shubhojit thought of walking back to his humble abode. He liked the casualness in the air and the novelty of not having a schedule or an itinerary of any kind.

'I'll come back soon and meet you, Ma,' he said, taking leave of his mother.

'Don't worry, Shubhojit,' said Kamladevi, 'let us have no formality. We can walk to each other's place, whenever we want. Let there be no time frame!'

Shubhojit came out of the haveli and started walking back along the same path. He walked slowly for about half a mile, and then sat under a bush, and watched the dusk setting in gently and quietly. He looked towards the settlement that was his village, and the grassy paths meandering through the wild landscape, going towards the village. As the natural light faded gradually and the birds were noisily returning to their nests, a single glint of light came up somewhere in a distant hut or mud structure. The villagers were welcoming the onset of night and preparing for rest after a hard day's labour.

The cattle too stood or sat motionless, wherever they found space or wherever they felt comfortable. A group of dogs lay casually on the outskirts of the village, one alert dog sending out a long bark at intervals.

Shubhojit smiled, got up, and took long strides to return home.

37

The sun had already set when Shubhojit reached his place and arranged his things in the somewhat low light. The unusual exercise had made him hungry and he longed for home food once again. His new home was equipped with all the basic necessities. Unlike his childhood when he would have to manage with a kerosene lantern, he had an electric connection here. He put the water to boil in the kettle while he sat on an easy chair in the veranda and surveyed the scene outside. There was a different kind of beauty in the untamed, wild landscape, which looked even more fascinating—although a bit intimidating—in the fading light of the day.

Shubhojit marvelled at the scene. He wondered at the natural formations of the rural areas. Many of the habitations, as far as he knew, were situated on the periphery of some kind of wilderness with a river or a canal nearby, and had a self-supporting survival system. Nature followed its own cycle but had been extremely generous to mankind. 'It is we people,' thought Shubhojit, 'who fail to connect with our surroundings and that has led to the severing of our natal sensations.'

The water in the kettle had been boiling for some time. The steam billowing out of its spout brought Shubhojit out of his reverie and he set about making a cup of tea for himself. He would think about his dinner a little later. Having a cup of his favourite tea in solitary surroundings had always been Shubhojit's favourite pastime. He came out with his tea to sit in the open. The cool breeze was blowing and Shubhojit could see the outline of the tall trees and shrubs even in the dark.

Shubhojit sipped his tea, enjoying its flavour and the right mixture of sugar and milk. Somewhere far off in the village, he could see dying embers which might have been from the smouldering chullahs which, earlier in the evening, must have been used for cooking the evening meal. As the fire died away, the swirls of smoke could still be seen rising in the sky. Shubhojit followed the smoke trail going upwards and vanishing, and saw the faint glimmer of stars that were quickly dotting the sky. Their increasing visibility made Shubhojit aware of the deepening darkness enveloping the houses. He remembered when the star-speckled sky used to fascinate him and his friends when they were growing up. They would spend countless hours gazing at the twinkling shimmer, trying to identify the stars, and recounting all the myths associated with them. The memory of those days brought back to his mind their endless conversations and the carefree games they played.

The cup of tea had refreshed his spirits and Shubhojit lazed in the chair for another half an hour before thinking of fixing his dinner. There was help in the nearby quarters, if he wanted, but Shubhojit would be able to take care of himself. He knew his mother would have left him some provisions for at least a day. He checked the kitchen shelves and the small refrigerator. There was plenty of milk, fruits and vegetables and also other items, such as chutney, butter, yogurt. Just then, there was a gentle knock and he saw two teenaged boys standing outside the door. One of them held a bowl in his hands.

'What brings you here, boys?' asked Shubhojit. 'And what are you carrying?'

'Good evening, Sir,' said one of them, 'we have been waiting for you since evening. Our grandmother has sent some khichdi for you. She thought you would like some light food for the evening meal.'

'Oh, thank you so much!' said Shubhojit, taking the bowl in his hands. 'Please tell your grandmother that I shall enjoy eating this. And, in future, I shall always ask for whatever I want. There is no formality. And yes, you may come over here whenever you want. I would love to go on excursions with you people or to the nearby bani.'

The boys touched his feet and went away.

Shubhojit decided to eat the steaming-hot khichdi right away. He placed it on the table and set about getting the other accompaniments. He knew it would taste good with yogurt and a little bit of butter. He could also fix himself a bowl of salad. Shubhojit was charged with the novelty of experience and he was enjoying being on his own. This was so different! He remembered the mealtimes at home with Yashodhra, Hemant and Neelakshi.

There was always a sense of urgency even when the children had grown up. The hustle and bustle during the meal would invariably be matched with a lavish spread of dishes, meant to suit everybody's tastes and likes.

When the children were young, they used to be interested in sharing their experiences with their parents. They would listen to their advice and act accordingly. As they grew up and their areas of interest widened, no amount of coaxing or scolding would force them to come out of their cocoon. Shubhojit, always busy and preoccupied, hardly had time for pampering them and he would lose his patience. This usually led to arguments. Then, Yashodhra resorted to giving the children dinner before Shubhojit came home. At times, he would barge into the dining room and object to their watching television while they were eating. He used to reprimand them for being constantly on their cell phones, even during the mealtime. These unsavoury incidents had led to a virtual snapping of communication among them till he fell sick when a greater sense of understanding had brought about a healthy relationship among them.

Shubhojit served himself some khichdi and came out again to sit in the veranda. That was the right place to inhale fresh air, look around and enjoy his food, bit by bit, mouthful by mouthful. He chewed his food slowly, gazed at the wonder of the blinking fireflies and admired the beauty of the rising moon in the fathomless sky.

He spent a long time on his dinner. He was in no hurry. He reclined on the chair after his meal was done and closed his eyes. There was a perfect stillness in the air and as he rested his head on his uplifted arms, he wondered whether the whole world had gone off to sleep. Even in that state of stupor, he could hear the slight rustle of the wind, or an occasional ripple in the water flowing nearby, or the random barking of a watchful dog somewhere in the distance.

Shubhojit remained in that half-awake, half-asleep state for some time. Thoughts raced in and out of his mind while his body rested and his nerves were calmed. He had lost count of time. He remained in this blessed state for about half an hour when his arms felt cramped and he came awake with a jolt. His reverie was broken and he became aware of his present surroundings. He remembered that he had eaten and the dishes needed to be taken care of. Shubhojit got up, did the needful and decided to take a stroll along the small canal. It would help him digest his food. He could come back after about an hour, put a cot in the veranda and sleep peacefully.

Shubhojit woke up the next morning to the chirping of birds. It was very early, even by his own standards. He had always been an early riser but city life had deprived him of the pleasure of sleeping outside in the open and being woken up by the pleasant sounds of nature. From the elders in his family, he had heard about the purity of morning air during the *Brahmvela*, that is, anywhere between three to half past four in the morning. According to the Hindu scriptures, this was the time when sages meditated and looked forward to their communion with God. Brahmvela could be interpreted as the hour of God and the perfect time for spiritual awakening.

Shubhojit was mesmerized by a subtle sacredness in the atmosphere. He felt overwhelmed; rather, somewhat intimidated by the incomprehensible mystery of the universe. There was certainly a difference between sleeping in a closed, air-conditioned room and sleeping out in the open. All intelligence, knowledge and wisdom descend on the human mind in the wee hours of the morning when it is at its best, and most receptive, thought Shubhojit. The nascent rays of the rising sun bestow their blessings on human beings at the crack of dawn. All creations of Nature, animate or inanimate, join their hands in extending a cheerful invitation to the world in the morning, sending a message of simplicity and innocence.

Could one wake up in better conditions, wondered Shubhojit. He felt that, through the night, he had been absorbing the natural sounds around him. They were now a part of his subconscious: the buzzing sound of insects, the rustle of wind, a murmur somewhere nearby in the grass, the whisper among the trees, the lovelorn cry of a solitary bird, and finally the wake-up call of the rooster.

It was many decades since Shubhojit had last heard the shrill but persistent call of nature's eternal but marvellous timekeeper. He got up and saw the wonderful, white rooster with a radiant *kalgi* (tuft), performing its duty diligently and determinedly, unmindful of the sleeping world around it. Shubhojit found its natural call to be a beautiful ode to the sheer beauty of the rising sun. Its continuing call in the wilderness was consistent, at measured intervals and of amazing precision. Shubhojit could only marvel at God's inimitable creation.

These simple and pleasant sounds should be enough for mankind, either to wake them up in the morning or lull them to sleep after a hard day's toil and labour. Perhaps, these too were governed by some simple logic which mankind was unable to understand, given the jet-set pace of civilization and its giant technological leaps.

'If only mankind would stop thinking business,' thought Shubhojit, 'at least for some time, and think of reconnecting with the natural environment, the world would become a much better place for simple living. If only the world would halt its one-upmanship and stem the tide of jealousy, hatred, dislike, pride, prejudice and greed! If only...' Shubhojit heaved a deep sigh.

He suddenly remembered what had been instilled in his mind during the formative years at school: 'Simple living and high thinking!'

'Our sages were right, our philosophers had hit upon the truth since times immemorial,' thought Shubhojit. 'We only have to go back to our vedas and listen to the voice of God. The greed for materialism has put an end to the process of spiritual awakening of mankind. Wordsworth, the eternal romantic, expressed it in his poem, *Lines Written in Early Spring,* where he laments:

> *If this belief from heaven be sent,*
> *If such be nature's holy plan,*
> *Have I not reason to lament,*
> *What man has made of man?*

Shubhojit loved the pastoral setting of his small place. His senses were already in an exhilarated state. He was able to see things that he had so far missed seeing; his sense of smell was perhaps sharper than before; his taste buds had become more discerning; he could hear the natural sounds all around him; and he was learning to enjoy them; he could feel empathy for his fellow beings and perceive what might not be otherwise apparent. In short, he had evolved as a born romantic who could think from the heart and feel with the mind.

And all this had happened to him in one night only. Shubhojit realized that this knowledge and these sensory perceptions were present in the minds and hearts of all men. But, they had lost awareness of it in the process of growing up or in the mad race for worldly acquisitions.

'I have come home now,' thought Shubhojit, 'to find peace and solitude; come home in search of my roots; and come home just in the nick of time! It is not too late!'

The scent of the soil had got the better of him while he had found the call of the wild irresistible! But for how long, he himself did not know!

Perhaps he could take a call after a year or so! Perhaps he would like to go back and finish his remaining responsibilities at home and workplace! Perhaps he would like to stay here for some more time! He would leave those decisions to be made spontaneously, thought Shubhojit, when it was the right time.

Shubhojit smiled and a deep sense of contentment radiated from his face.

It was spring time for him now!

He didn't want to miss the beauty and sanctity of the moment at any cost!

He had come a long way for this!

Made in the USA
Monee, IL
04 May 2026